Buzz
Honey

100%
Honey

ALL PURPOSE

IKOMAN

Soy Sauce

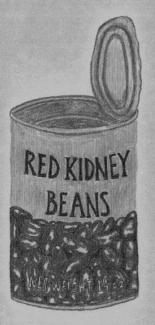

RED KIDNEY
BEANS

NET WEIGHT 14 OZ

Tuong An Pho
HOISIN SAUCE

WT./CAN NANG 20

DECECCO

DECECCO Spaghetti no 12

BURNT
TOAST
AND OTHER
DISASTERS

ALSO BY CAL PETERNELL

Almonds, Anchovies, and Pancetta

A Recipe for Cooking

Twelve Recipes

BURNT TOAST

AND OTHER

DISASTERS

A BOOK OF HEROIC HACKS,
FABULOUS FIXES, AND SECRET SAUCES

CAL PETERNELL

wm

WILLIAM MORROW

An Imprint of HarperCollins*Publishers*

FOR EVERY COOK
WHO CONJURES IN FRIDGE LIGHT,
RUMMAGES DARK CABINETS,
PULLS OUT THEIR SCRAPPY SKILLETS
AND POCKED POTS TO MAKE US
SOMETHING DELICIOUS

CONTENTS

INTRODUCTION 1

TIPS: THINGS YOU SHOULD KNOW FOR GOOD COOKING 5

BURNT 13

BURNT TOAST: Onion Panade; Cheesy Onion Bread Pudding; *REALLY* ROASTED VEGETABLES: Roasted Vegetable Cornmeal Cakes; Roasted Vegetable Salad with Ginger, Lime, and Sour Cream; Roasted Vegetable Salad with Figgy Dressing; *REALLY* BOILED VEGETABLES; *REALLY* WELL-DONE MEATS: Turkey Etcetrazzini with Chicken, Beef, Pork, and Lamb Variations; MUSHY RICE: Coconut Rice Pudding with Ginger; Mushy Rice Pancakes

HACKING PACKAGES 35

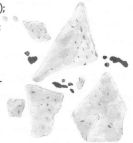

POPCORN; INSTANT SOUP, A LOVE STORY: Vegetable Soup with Cauliflower, Apple, Peas, and Spices, Knorr Version; Vegetable Soup with Cauliflower, Apple, Peas, and Spices, Scratch Version; HACKARONI AND CHEESE; CAN OF BEANS, MASH-UP FRY-UPS, SALADS, AND SAUCES: The Mitts-Full MUFU: Can of Corn *and* Can of Black Beans; White Bean MUFU: Tuscan Style; The Garbonanza MUFU: Chickpea with Turmeric and Cilantro; Red Bean MUFU: Smoky Style; Cannellini Bean and Celery Salad with Anchovies; Can of Beans Cooked with Rice and Lots of Scallions and Cilantro; Chickpeas with Tomato, Rosemary, and Cream; SARDINE AND ANCHOVY S'COOL: Spaghetti with Cream, Garlic, and Anchovies; Pasta with Sardines; HAMBURG-A-RONI: Campfire Edition; EGGS: Tortilla Española on Vacation

WHAT THEY SHOULDA DONE 63

NACHOS, TWO WAYS: Nachos with Queso Fundido (Molten Cheese); My Cakes, Nacho Cakes; Milo's Bean Dip; DRESSINGS: Ranch Dressing; Caesar Salad Dressing; NOT-PESTOS: Marjoram Walnut Not-Pesto; Arugula Almond Not-Pesto; Cilantro Peanut Not-Pesto; Mint Pistachio Not-Pesto; UNTHICK CLAM CHOWDER: New England Version, Diner Edition

SCHMEGETABLES 81

Brocco Tacos; Regular Onions with Hoisin and Shaoxing Wine; ONION
RINGINGS: Skaket Beach Thins; Yogurt Rings; Gluten-Free Not-Rings; Celery
Swooshes with Peanuts and Ginger; Mushrooms with Honey and Coriander;
Celery Baked with Black Pepper, Bacon, and Cream; Roasted Radishes with Chiles,
Lime, and Fish Sauce; Glazed Carrot Phalanges (a.k.a. Baby Carrots); Carrots
Roasted in the Aftermath; Mess of Scallions; Scallion Dip; Baked Potatoes and
Surrogate Fries

MEAT NOT CUTE 105

BS CHICKEN THIGHS: Dijon Chicken Thighs Royale; Chipotle Chicken Thighs with
Cumin and Honey; Creamy Chicken Ragù: Cheese Grater Edition; BS CHICKEN BREAST,
EASY-FRIED TWO WAYS: BS Chicken Breast, Dorato-Style; BS Chicken Breast, Tangy
and Turmerical; Spice-Encrusted BS Chicken Breast Roast; GRAVY, MEATLOAF, AND
MEATBALLS: Gravy; Hot-Patootie Meatloaf; Mushroom Meatballs

SPECIAL SAUCES FOR THE BORING 125

VEGETABLE PUREES; SMASHED BEANS; NUT SALSAS AND SAUCES;
YOGURT SAUCES; THE CREAM: Penne in Pink; Creamy Cabbage with
Caraway Seeds, Dill, and Hot Pepper; Creamy Sweet Peppers with Seeds
Not Their Own; Dip of Fools; BUTTER: Brown Butters; Butter Pan Sauce;
Compound Butters

CODA: A COLLECTION OF DRINKS TO FORGET YOU BY 151

Acknowledgments 157
Universal Conversion Chart 159
Index 161

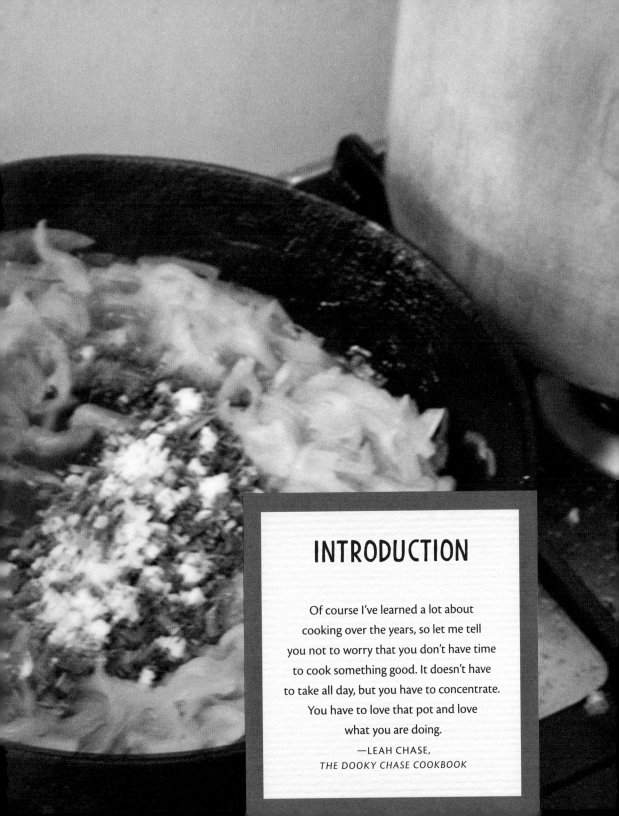

INTRODUCTION

Of course I've learned a lot about
cooking over the years, so let me tell
you not to worry that you don't have time
to cook something good. It doesn't have
to take all day, but you have to concentrate.
You have to love that pot and love
what you are doing.

—LEAH CHASE,
THE DOOKY CHASE COOKBOOK

It is very calming, this thinking about, inventing, preparing, and eating food. Anything to do with food sets off reveries and memories and brilliant conceits while releasing floods of endorphins to take away pain.

—JAMES HAMILTON-PATERSON,
COOKING WITH FERNET BRANCA

A mistake is a bad thing only until it is fixed, at which point it becomes not only good, but magic: mistakes are the swept-up stardust that success sparkles with. This, then, is a cookbook full of just such success stories, of bad food made good. It's a book about moving the dial, about meeting food where it is and bringing it someplace better, regardless of the why of it. Maybe the thing you bought isn't as good as you'd hoped and it needs help. Or the thing is fine, but you messed it up! Maybe you have limited things, limited time, limited budget. Did you get the same old thing and are hungry to sauce it up? Are you going broke ordering takeout, and anyway, you feel like you could make it better yourself, or at least you'd like to try? Did you burn the figurative toast? The actual toast? Success is at hand.

When my parents were more mobile, and my young family was younger, they used to visit us in California. We never had a house big enough for them to stay with us, which was probably a good thing, but they would come for dinners, proud of their chef son if sometimes confused by the things he would cook, the enthusiastic friends he'd invite, the tumbledown state of his house and kitchen. Now, traveling is too difficult for them, so I make dinners in their kitchen when I visit

them in South Carolina. They always ask what I would like to cook, and I always give my standard response: Let's find what looks good at the market and I will plan around that. But what, I wondered one day as we drove from Walmart to Piggly Wiggly to Publix, if nothing looks particularly good? Despair soon turned to inspiration as I grabbed butter and beans and broccoli, and *Burnt Toast and Other Disasters* was born.

It was during that visit, and other trips outside the bubble I admittedly live in, that I began to realize a major flaw in the way I have always approached cooking. Though it is indisputable that the very best ingredients make the very best food, access to those ingredients is not shared by all. Which I knew. My mistake: not well enough. I've been a lucky one, with a career full of cooking fantastic ingredients, confident that, with a steady seasoning hand and stream of good olive oil, success was all but assured. When asked, "What did you do to that . . . salmon . . . green bean . . . tomato . . . to make it *sooo* delicious?!" I'd tell the truth, that I'd simply brought together the trinity of good olive oil, a little salt, and great . . . salmon or green bean or tomato. I'd marvel at the surprise bordering on indignant disbelief I'd be met with. Why was that so hard to understand? I'd think, growing indignant myself. Of course, I was the one who didn't understand. Here's why: Within a hundred miles of where I live are some of the best farms, ranches, fishing grounds, vineyards, artisan bakers, and cheesemakers in the world! I'd be one foolish chef to not bring these local ingredients together without getting too much in their way, especially with the access that running a restaurant like Chez Panisse affords.

My former boss and mentor, Alice Waters, likes to tell the story of a time when she was one of several chefs contributing dishes to a large fundraising event. Upon seeing the colorful, simple, perfect salad Alice had made, a fellow chef commented, "That's not cooking, that's shopping!" He thought he was dishing, but Alice took it as high praise, acknowledgment of the importance that she, and so many of her acolytes, places on the careful sourcing of ingredients.

But too often the shopping's not so good: the measly side-strip of factory-farmed produce at the giant grocery chain, the slim pickings at the convenience store. We've all been there, and it's where good recipes come in—a kind of cooking that, despite decades of kitchen experience, I had to teach myself. The resulting shifts in perspective revealed that there was a lot I didn't know in, and out of, the kitchen. Grateful to the many who've taught me so generously, I hope here to pass on the favor.

If this is starting to sound like a Sullivan's Culinary Travels, Mr. Cheffy-Pants Goes to Walmart sort of thing, I promise that is not what lies ahead. I know I'm not the person to write a cookbook about what it's like to have bad access to good food, but I believe I *am* the guy to write about how to take what you've got and make it taste, look, and feel good. I know that *every* level of cooking can be improved, that the humblest can be delicious, the good made great. So, if some overcooked rice, an onion, and the condiment shelf are all we've got for dinner . . . or if the vegetables

drawer is full, but full of the perfectly fine but same old stuff that you're bored with . . . or if you, or she, or he, or they missed lunch and now you are all in a hurry and hangry . . . let's see what we can do! Naturally, you're not going to *try* for bad situations or bad ingredients— these recipes will also work with ingredients of the best quality—but things happen, and here's this cookbook for when you need a fixer. I am not presuming to be any kind of savior, other than the kind that anyone is when they bring good, tasty food to the table at the end of a hard day.

That said, I do think we should all be eating better foods, and I know that it's possible—we have the farmland that can produce the nutritious and beautiful foods that everyone needs and loves. But just as important is that we eat good-*tasting* food, recognizing that there's value in the pleasure we get from cooking and eating delicious meals, whether they come straight from the farm or from a convenience store shelf. It's reality cooking, not aspirational but always tasty.

These recipes are going to pull you out of the Wednesday weeds and into the Saturday sunshine. They'll make your bad into good and your good into better. Taking inspiration from disappointment, *Burnt Toast and Other Disasters* is a bag of tricks for turning supermarket-standard into a supper to be proud of. Hopefully you'll find some of these recipes so good that you'll be making intentional mistakes that start to look, and taste, a lot like successes.

TIPS: THINGS YOU SHOULD KNOW FOR GOOD COOKING

"We give advice by the bucket,
but take it by the grain."
—TOM STOPPARD

Here's my bucket of kitchen advice. I've underlined some grains that I especially hope you'll take (for skillets, cooking oils, garlic, spices, nuts, seeds, and meats).

MY ESSENTIAL EQUIPMENT

- **Three knives:** chef's, paring, and serrated/bread
- **Cutting board:** preferably wood and definitely not glass
- **Box grater:** one, max, of the sides should be starry

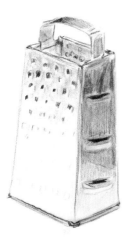

- **Metal spatula:** thin, not thick, not plastic-coated
- **Other utensils:** wooden spoons, ladle, rubber spatula, whisk, and can opener
- **Measuring cups and spoons**
- **Tongs:** hinged on the end, not in the middle like scissors
- **Peeler:** essential for stripping away mistake parts of things (apples, roots, spuds, and so on). I like Y-shaped peelers of the cheapest sort.

- **Mortar and pestle or grinder for spices:** Either is fine, but you can't grind spices in the same grinder you use for coffee, obviously, and a mortar and pestle are a lot to handle when grinding coffee before you've *had* coffee so . . . both? Or drink tea.
- **Pots:** big pot, medium pot
- **Colander:** for draining pasta and rice and beans. Avoid plastic, which can leach toxins when exposed to heat, especially hot liquids.
- **Large skillet:** When I need a nonstick surface, like for eggs, I use cast iron. For everything else it's cast iron or heavy stainless steel. (Used cast iron is often better in terms of price, quality, and seasoning. All-Clad will last forever, is expensive, and is worth it.) If you have a thinner skillet, using lower heat for a longer time will help prevent scorching.
- **Blender:** not the cheapest sort, if possible. Immersion blenders are very handy for pureeing soups, etc., and arguably less good for milkshakes and cocktails.
- **Spider strainer:** for lifting foods out of hot water or oil; also good for pressing boiled eggs or avocadoes through. Look for the bamboo-handled wire type, often available inexpensively in Chinatown markets.
- **Baking sheet**
- **Timer:** for not-burning. Also for burning but not *burning*!
- **Casserole dish**

COMMON INGREDIENTS AND HOW TO USE THEM

- **Cooking oils:** I try to have two kinds of olive oil on hand, because while swirling the best extra-virgin oil onto a salad or garlicky grilled bread is a great idea, pouring it into a hot skillet is an unnecessary indulgence. For that, use a neutral olive or vegetable oil, or do what I do and make a blend using one part fancy olive oil to three or four parts canola, grapeseed, or other vegetable oil.
- **Garlic:** Raw garlic in considered amounts should be very finely grated or crushed/chopped to a paste with a pinch of salt, either by mortar and pestle or with a knife on a cutting board.
- **Parsley:** Italian flat-leaf parsley works best, washed and dried, leaves picked from stems, and finely chopped.
- **Cilantro** is better roughly chopped, stems and all, after washing and drying.
- **Hard herbs** like rosemary, sage, savory, and thyme should be used in small amounts when raw, leaves picked from stems and finely chopped. Frying them in shallow oil first allows more generous use—the herbs are left mellowed and crisped. The oil, I find, is no longer good for eating but can be saved for the next herb-frying.

- **Spices** stay their most fresh and flavorful if bought whole-seed. Toast them before using to bring out their best: Heat a small skillet over medium heat and add the spices. When they start to hop around a little and smell spicy, shake the pan and toast for 15 seconds. Crush in a mortar and pestle or spice mill, or with the bottom of a heavy pan on a cutting board. Pre-ground spices do not require toasting but lose their sparkle more quickly, so use them up before they do.

- **Nuts** are prone to spoilage; keep them sealed in the freezer and taste them before use. Toast in a 350°F oven until lightly browned on the inside, about 10 minutes—set a timer and cut a nut in two to check doneness. Chopping nuts can be a little like cat-herding (which, outside of idioms, no one does; see Wanda Gág's brilliant and brutal *Millions of Cats* for the exception). As a workaround, I run the nuts over with a rolling pin first so they don't fly all over while I'm chopping.

- **Sesame seeds:** Buy them already toasted or heat a skillet over medium heat and add the sesame seeds. Toast, stirring and tossing, until they are lightly browned and fragrant, 3 to 5 minutes. Put on a plate to cool.

- **Turmeric as remedy:** I get annoyed hearing that this or that food is supposed to be "good for you." What does it mean? Could there ever really be a food that is simply good for you, regardless of your age, size, health, circumstance, needs, desires, no matter what? Of course not! Then, turmeric. The color, obviously. The incredible strength *and* enveloping softness. Powdered, it's pigment, marking you healthy as sunshine. Fresh, it's a glow stick, so fresh you slap your

paprika

turmeric

own face and then hurry and get some more. Mira Nair, the brilliant director, once showed me how to make the delicious chai that she drinks like it's "on a drip," but what she really wanted to talk about was haldi doodh, the mixture of hot milk and turmeric that her aunties, and everyone, say is the remedy for . . . everything. She'd been cooking up plenty of it lately to help her bones knit back together, having literally broken a leg at the Berkeley Rep Theatre, where she was directing *Monsoon Wedding* for the stage. And turmeric can do even more than heal geniuses. Whenever something needs a visual boost, turmeric can help: pale soups, gray stews, blended vegetables (page 126); beans (pages 48 and 129); batter for frying (page 89); or spice-coating for chicken (page 115).

- **Croutons:** Don't forget how good croutons can make a salad or a bowl of soup. And really, so many things can play the crouton role—toasted scraps of bread, bagels, or pitas, of course, but also pretzels, toasted tortillas or tortilla chips, crackers. I'll even add, without reservation but not without restraint, potato chips, Goldfish . . . maybe not Cheetos or Fritos, but . . . your call. See the Toast chapter in my first book, *Twelve Recipes*, for more on doing delicious things with croutons and toasts.
- **Bread crumbs:**
  - A 1-pound loaf with crust carved off will make 7 cups of fresh bread crumbs.
  - Overtoasted bread, dry hard bread, and the dried-out crusts from fresh loaves can be ground in a food processor or blender to make dry bread crumbs.

coriander

cumin

fennel

- **Meats:**
  ....
  - Grass-fed beef and organic/sustainable meats cost more, but seem worth it. I offset the cost by eating less of them.
  - Anything touched by raw meat—your hands, knives, cutting boards, platters—must be washed before anything else touches it.
  - Meats are better when seasonings, especially salt, are applied well before cooking. Big things like roasts and whole chickens are best when seasoned and refrigerated an hour or three before cooking.
  - Unless you're in a big hurry, meat should be allowed to come to room temperature before cooking—somewhere not in hot sunlight, and where the dog or other critters won't start in on it.
  - The best way to tell when meat is done is to cut in a little, with a sharp knife in a discreet spot, and take a peek.

- Meats can—and, in the case of larger, sliceable cuts, should—rest in a warm place while you finish preparing the rest of the meal.
- **Parmesan and Grana Padano:** Parmigiano-Reggiano is expensive, worth it, and replaceable with also-very-good Grana Padano when needed.
- <u>Used oils/grease:</u> Otherwise sensible people pour grease down the drain. Don't do that! Here's what I do:
  - If it's bacon grease, chicken fat, or the like, I pour it, or some of it, over my dog Benny's kibble, which he then appreciates much more.
- If Benny's coat is getting almost *too* glossy (and a little tight), I put the grease in an empty milk carton and freeze it until compost pickup day. Sometimes I use an empty can, freeze it, and guiltily put it in the trash.
- If there is a lot, like if I have been deep-frying, I let the oil cool, funnel it back into the bottle, and take it to the local recycling place, where they use it to make biodiesel.

BURNT

Often calamity turns to our advantage and
great ruins make way for greater glories.
—SENECA THE YOUNGER

First of all, burnt is not always a bad thing. Consider, for example, everyone's favorite barbecue delicacy, bragging with its very name that where the burnt ends, the delicious begins. Other popular burnt fare includes scallions, butter, popcorn, caramel, marshmallows on sticks, roux, tomatoes and peppers for mole or romesco, the prime pickings around the edge of a pan of almost anything . . . there's a lot to like. Inevitably, though, there are times—smoking-toaster, ruined-pot, oven-on-fire times—when dinner's not caramelized, charred, or blackened; it's plain throw-it-away burnt.

Second of all, "burnt" can mean boiled, wiggly, and wan rather than hard and charred.

Toothless pasta, mushy rice, flabby spuds—soup was invented from these, the primordial soup of soup. Simply dumping the drowned, swollen spaghetti into the blender, water and all, does not, however, a great soup make. But a passable soup could be made by pureeing that spaghetti with some or all of the sauce you had ready. Or save the sauce for another time and cook some onions or leeks, add whatever herbs or spices are at hand, and spin the lot with all the washed-up pasta, *some* of the salty, starchy, cooking water, and a little butter, yogurt, cream, or olive oil. If you have some parsley or cilantro to chop, or something crunchy to crumble on top, it'll be almost like you meant to do that.

BURNT TOAST

You know what to do if you burn a piece of toast—scrape it and butter it or scrap it and try again. But when you burn a trayful in the oven or serially burn slices in your toaster, and they're not *too* blackened, you can save them to grind fine in the blender or food processor to use in meatloaf/ball recipes, to thicken soups, or to mix with olive oil (and garlic, anchovies, and red pepper flakes!) and toss with hot spaghetti. Or don't grind them and make the simple and delicious onion panade or savory, cheesy bread pudding that follows.

ONION PANADE

If you have homemade stock, make panade. The onions, well-cooked but not browned, counter the bread's overtoastiness.

MAKES 6 SERVINGS

¼ cup olive or vegetable oil (or a combination of oil and butter), plus more for the baking dish

3 large yellow onions, thinly sliced

1 teaspoon fine sea salt or kosher salt

Ground black pepper

2 teaspoons chopped fresh thyme leaves or sage leaves (optional)

6 cups good chicken stock

12 to 16 ounces very much toasted bread (about a loaf's worth)

4 ounces cheese (Gruyère, Cheddar, and/or Gouda), grated

2 tablespoons butter, cut into thin slices

Heat a large skillet (see Tips, page 6) over high heat and add the oil, then the onions and ½ teaspoon of the salt. Stir until the onions get going, then reduce the heat to medium and cook, stirring occasionally, until the onions are soft and very lightly browned, 15 to 20 minutes. Cover with a lid or add a splash of water if the onions color too much before getting soft. Add some black pepper and the thyme or sage, if using, and cook a minute more. Set aside.

Heat the oven to 400°F.

Bring the stock to a boil in a large pot over high heat, add the remaining ½ teaspoon salt, and keep hot over low heat while you build the panade. Brush a 3-quart baking dish or casserole or a large cast-iron pan with oil, and then fit in a layer of bread, breaking up the slices as necessary to fill in any gaps. Arrange a third of the onions over the bread and sprinkle with a quarter of the cheese. Repeat until there are four layers of bread and three of filling (set aside the final quarter of the cheese). Press the layers down with your hands and then pour in enough hot stock to just reach the top layer. Cover with foil and bake until very hot in the middle, about 45 minutes.

Remove the foil, dot with butter, sprinkle with the remaining cheese, and return to the oven until bubbling and browned on top, 25 to 30 minutes. The panade should be quite wet under the top crust, almost soupy. Add leftover hot stock if needed to make it so.

Scoop into bowls and eat hot.

CHEESY ONION BREAD PUDDING

Hearty, good, and, especially if you go for the meat option, like a sandwich casserole. Eat with restraint and pickles.

MAKES 6 SERVINGS

2 tablespoons cooking oil, olive or vegetable (see Tips, page 7), plus more for the baking dish

2 tablespoons butter

2 large yellow onions

1 teaspoon fine sea salt or kosher salt

2 garlic cloves, chopped

1 tablespoon chopped fresh thyme, tarragon, or sage leaves (optional)

3 eggs

1 cup light or heavy cream

2 cups whole milk

1 teaspoon Dijon mustard

Ground black pepper

12 to 16 ounces very much toasted bread (about a loaf's worth)

4 ounces cheese (Gruyère, Cheddar, and/or Gouda), grated

2 tablespoons chopped fresh parsley leaves (optional)

6 ounces sliced ham, salami, or coppa, cut in approximately ½-inch squares (optional)

Heat a large skillet (see Tips, page 6) over high heat and add the oil and butter, then the onions and ½ teaspoon of the salt. Stir until the onions get going, then reduce the heat to medium and cook, stirring occasionally, until the onions are soft and very lightly browned, 15 to 20 minutes. Cover with a lid or add a splash of water if the onions color too much before getting soft. Add the garlic and herbs, if using, and cook a minute more. Set aside.
Heat the oven to 375°F.
In a large bowl, whisk together the eggs, cream, milk, mustard, pepper, and remaining ½ teaspoon salt until completely combined. Break up the toast into the mixture and add the onion mixture, three quarters of the cheese, and the parsley and ham, if using. Use your hands to stir everything together very well, then turn into a greased 3-quart casserole dish or the skillet you cooked the onions in if it is oven-safe. Bake, uncovered, until browned, bubbly, and hot in the center, about 40 minutes. Sprinkle with the reserved cheese and bake another 10 minutes.

Variation

In place of, or in addition to, the ham, salami, or coppa, stir chopped (over)roasted vegetables into the mixture.

REALLY ROASTED VEGETABLES

Every time I roast vegetables, some—the ones around the edges at least—get a little, or a lot, burnt. Everyone fights over them. If the lot has gone dark—if, for example, I forgot to set my trusty wind-up timer—I use one of these treatments and it's feast, not fight.

- Squeeze on lime juice and sprinkle with Marash pepper for stand-around-the-kitchen snacking.

- Serve with any one of the yogurt sauces (page 134) as either a dressing or a dip.
- Chop and cook into your favorite tomato sauce for pasta! I like adding *really* roasted vegetables to all'arrabbiata sauce (tomato with garlic and crushed red pepper flakes) or al Claudia sauce (tomato with onions, capers, and lemon zest).
- Mix into Cheesy Onion Bread Pudding (page 17).

ROASTED VEGETABLE CORNMEAL CAKES

This makes enough batter for a baking tray amount of vegetables that roasted too far. Delicious with eggs, alongside meats or fish, or with any of the bean MUFUs (pages 46–50). Nice with a dollop of sour cream or one of the yogurt sauces (page 134). My son Liam demonstrated to me that these are also good with maple syrup.

MAKES 8 TO 10 THREE-INCH CAKES

½ cup all-purpose flour

½ cup cornmeal

2 teaspoons baking soda

½ teaspoon fine sea salt or kosher salt

1 egg

¾ cup whole milk

2 tablespoons unsalted butter, melted

2 scallions, green *and* white parts, thinly sliced

2 cups *Really* Roasted Vegetables (page 18)

Cooking oil, olive or vegetable (see Tips, page 7)

Put a baking sheet in the oven and heat to 200°F for keeping the cornmeal cakes warm as you fry in batches.

In a large bowl, mix the flour, cornmeal, baking soda, and salt together. In a separate bowl, lightly beat the egg and milk together. Stir into the flour mixture until fully combined, then add the melted butter, scallions, and roasted vegetables. Stir well and set aside.

Heat a large skillet (see Tips, page 6) over medium heat, add a coating of oil, and add spoonfuls of the batter, working in batches as needed. Flip the cakes when bubbles begin to form in the middles, after about 4 minutes. Cook the other sides until browned, 2 to 3 minutes, then hold them in the warm oven while you cook the rest.

ROASTED VEGETABLE SALAD WITH GINGER, LIME, AND SOUR CREAM

Sour can trump (a perfectly good word that we need to take back! Or . . . never speak again?) bitter-burnt, hence lime and sour cream.

MAKES 6 SERVINGS

3 scallions, green *and* white parts, thinly sliced, or 1 shallot, thinly sliced

1 small garlic clove, grated or pounded to a paste (see Tips, page 7)

½ inch of fresh ginger, grated (about 1 teaspoon)

¼ teaspoon fine sea salt or kosher salt

Juice of 1 lime

1 teaspoon white or red vinegar

3 tablespoons olive oil

4 cups *Really* Roasted Vegetables (page 18)

Handful of fresh cilantro, mint, and/or basil leaves

¼ cup sour cream or crème fraîche, thinned with enough water or milk to make it thickly pourable

Marash, Urfa, or Aleppo pepper to taste

Make the vinaigrette: In a small bowl, stir together the scallions, garlic, ginger, salt, lime juice, vinegar, and olive oil. Taste and adjust the vinaigrette with more . . . salt, lime, oil?

In a large bowl, combine the roasted vegetables, herbs, and most of the vinaigrette and toss to coat well. Taste and adjust, then spread out on a platter. Drizzle with the remaining dressing and the thinned sour cream. Sprinkle with the pepper.

Variation

Finely chop the vegetables and add more sour cream and herbs to make a dip for chips or raw vegetables.

ROASTED VEGETABLE SALAD WITH FIGGY DRESSING

Sweet figs do nice things for bitter-burnt things. This dressing is also good spooned over roasted pork or chicken that needs a little something, and tossed with hearty salad greens like radicchio, escarole, or frisée.

MAKES ⅓ CUP DRESSING

1 small shallot, finely diced, or 1 scallion, green *and* white parts, thinly sliced

Fine sea salt or kosher salt

3 teaspoons red wine vinegar or balsamic vinegar or both in equal parts

1 teaspoon Dijon mustard

Ground black pepper

2 or 3 dried figs, soaked in hot water until soft (about 30 minutes), finely chopped

¼ cup olive oil

4 cups *Really* Roasted Vegetables (page 18)

Make the vinaigrette: In a small bowl, stir together the shallots, salt, vinegar, mustard, and pepper and let sit for a few minutes to allow the shallots to temper in the vinegar. Stir in the figs and the olive oil. Taste and adjust the vinaigrette with more . . . salt, vinegar, oil?
In a large bowl, dress the roasted vegetables with most of the vinaigrette and toss to coat well. Taste and adjust, then spread out on a platter. Drizzle with the remaining dressing if you like.

REALLY BOILED VEGETABLES

Chefs I know love boiled vegetables: salted water rolling energetically, the freshest vegetables of the season, cooked till they taste right and dressed with something simple like good olive oil or butter, a dab of nice miso or tahini . . . what's not to love? But those same chefs run into a little trouble making converts of those for whom boiled vegetables means something very different. I've heard them (okay, me) saying things like "cooked in salted water" or "blanched" to little effect. The truth is that boiled is boiled and overboiled is a problem. Good news—you need little more than an onion and a blender to fix it.

If you've overboiled a little bit of vegetables, well . . . maybe just toss them? Or you could try draining them very well and spinning them in the blender or food processor with some olive oil and a little garlic that's been finely grated or pounded with salt (see Tips, page 7), or just throw a raw clove in the blender but be sure it gets completely ground up. Spread the mixture on toast, or see page 126 for more suggested uses.

If there's more than a little bit of vegetables, make them into a delicious soup:

- Drain the vegetables and set aside. Save the water, or some of it, for the soup broth.
- Thinly slice a medium yellow onion.
- Cook the onion with salt and 4 tablespoons (¼ cup) butter or cooking oil (olive or vegetable) over medium-low heat until very soft, about 15 minutes.
- Add chopped garlic or ginger, spices, herbs, or all of these and cook until smelling great, about half a minute.
- Add the vegetables and just enough of the cooking water to cover—you can always thin it later.
- If you have old bread, cooked potatoes, or cooked rice, add some; they will give body and suavity. A glug of cream? Same. Stream of olive oil? Yes, please.
- Bring to a simmer to unite the flavors. Let cool at least a bit, then carefully blend it smooth in batches—don't overfill the blender with soup, especially if the soup is still hot.
- You can pass the puree through a fine strainer to make it extra smooth. Taste and correct with . . . salt, vinegar, lemon or lime juice, more of the cooking water if it is too thick, more cream or olive oil if it's too lean.

REALLY WELL-DONE MEATS

Some meats, like those from animals' edges—tails, cheeks, shanks—are at their very best when you cook the heck out of them. But here we are talking about cuts from the middles, the ones that you *wanted* cooked medium or even rare but instead cooked well. *Very* well. And now what you have is a dry problem, or a tough problem, or a very tough, dry problem.

My fix for the roast, steak, or breast that is woefully overcooked may seem counterintuitive: cook it more. It's really just a one-two-three template with endless variation:

1. Slice the meat thin.
2. Layer it with flavorful stuff.
3. Add liquid and bake.

You may have to do this tomorrow, unless you don't mind eating really late tonight, so have a nice omelet or a bowl of cereal (or see Popcorn and other recipes in Hacking Packages, page 35).

These recipes are for 1 to 1½ pounds of cooked meat. Meats can be switched out among the variations. The basic method is the same for them all.

TURKEY ETCETRAZZINI

A take on the Black Friday classic—feel free to toss in any etceteras (green beans, Brussels sprouts, greens) that are spilling out of your post-holiday fridge.

MAKES 4 SERVINGS

2 tablespoons cooking oil, olive or vegetable (see Tips, page 7)

2 tablespoons unsalted butter

1 pound mushrooms, rinsed (if needed) and thickly sliced or quartered

1 medium yellow onion, diced

1 teaspoon fine sea salt or kosher salt

6 thyme sprigs, leaves picked from stems and chopped

1 bay leaf

½ cup dry white wine, or a combination of dry white wine and sherry (or Shaoxing wine)

½ cup light or heavy cream or sour cream or crème fraîche (but not half-and-half; it will break)

1 to 1½ pounds overcooked turkey, or leftover turkey that's a bit dry, cut in ¼-inch slices

1 pound pasta (optional)

Heat the oven to 375°F.

Heat a large skillet (see Tips, page 6) to high and add the oil and butter. As soon as the butter melts, add the mushrooms, onion, and salt. Cook, stirring occasionally, until the mushrooms are browned and the onion tender, 10 to 15 minutes. Add the thyme and bay leaf and stir for 20 seconds. Add the wine, bring to a simmer, and cook for a minute. Add the cream and 1½ cups water, and increase the heat to high and bring to a simmer.

If the skillet can go in the oven, tuck the slices of turkey in with the onion and mushrooms. Otherwise, spread the turkey slices in a baking dish and pour the onion-mushroom mixture over them. Bake until the turkey is very tender, about 1 hour, checking at the half hour mark to see if you might need to add some water to keep it soupy.

Use a spoon to break up the larger pieces of turkey if you're going to toss with noodles (which you can now boil in salted water); otherwise serve as is like a stew, or with rice, potatoes, toast, and a salad or vegetable.

Cheesy Chicken Etcetrazzini

Heat the oven to 375°F.

Find 2 cups of tomato sauce, yours or jarred, and use half of it to cover the bottom of a baking dish. If you have fresh herbs, such as parsley, basil, and/or cilantro, roughly chop them and scatter over the sauce. Slice the overcooked chicken breast thinly and arrange the slices in the dish. Grind on some black pepper and cover with the remaining tomato sauce. Add enough water, or cream, or a combination, to keep things moist and juicy while the chicken bakes—it shouldn't be flooded, just sort of swampy. Drizzle with olive oil and sprinkle with grated cheese—mozzarella is great, but Cheddar, provolone, or lots of Parmesan will work.

Cover with foil and bake for 30 minutes. Uncover and continue baking until the cheese gets browned and bubbly, about 15 minutes. Add more water if it seems to be getting dry at all.

Serve with bread or toast, polenta, or set atop pasta simply dressed with olive oil.

Herby Beef Etcetrazzini

Heat the oven to 375°F.

Slice or dice a yellow onion and cook it in a large skillet over medium heat with ¼ cup olive or vegetable oil and a sprinkle of salt. Stir occasionally and, when tender, add minced garlic; sweet, smoked, or hot paprika; black pepper; red pepper flakes; and fresh herbs if possible (thyme, savory . . . dried oregano too). Add a glass of white or red wine, ½ cup cream or sour cream or crème fraîche, and enough water or stock to just cover. Increase the heat to bring to a simmer.

If the skillet can go in the oven, thinly slice the beef and tuck the slices in with the onion mixture. Otherwise, spread the slices in a baking dish and pour the onion mixture over them. Bake until the beef is tender and stewy, adding more liquid if needed, about 1 hour.

Good with buttered noodles or mashed potatoes.

Vindaloo-Style Pork Etcetrazzini

Heat the oven to 375°F.

Slice or dice a yellow onion and cook it in a large skillet over medium heat with ¼ cup olive or vegetable oil and a sprinkle of salt. Stir occasionally until tender, 10 to 15 minutes. Meanwhile, slice the pork, preferably across the grain.

Add a chopped garlic clove or two to the skillet and stir for 20 seconds, then add 4 dried dates, pitted and chopped, or 2 heaping tablespoons raisins; 2 teaspoons cumin seeds, crushed or ground (see Tips, page 8); ⅛ teaspoon ground cloves (1 clove's worth, if grinding yourself); 1 teaspoon sweet paprika; 2 teaspoons turmeric; crushed red pepper flakes to taste; ¼ cup red wine vinegar or cider vinegar (or more if you like sour); and 2 cups water. Increase the heat to bring to a simmer.

If the skillet can go in the oven, tuck the slices of pork in with the onion. Otherwise, spread the pork slices in a baking dish and pour the onion mixture over them. Bake until the pork is very tender, about 1 hour, checking at the half hour mark to see if you might need to add some water to keep it soupy.

Delicious with rice and a cucumber-radish salad and lots of fresh cilantro; with peanut salsa (page 130); or with a yogurt sauce (page 134).

Lamb Leg Etcetrazzini

Heat the oven to 375°F.

Slice or dice a yellow onion and cook in a large skillet over medium heat with ¼ cup olive or vegetable oil and a sprinkle of salt. Stir occasionally and, when tender, add sliced or chopped garlic; 1 can anchovies, drained and chopped; fresh herbs, if possible, like thyme or sage or rosemary; crushed red pepper flakes; a little chopped tomato or tomato paste; and a glass of white wine. Add 2 cups water and increase the heat to bring to a simmer.

If the skillet can go in the oven, tuck the slices of lamb in with the onion. Otherwise, spread the lamb slices in a baking dish and pour the onion mixture over them. Bake until the lamb is very tender, about 1 hour, checking at the half hour mark to see if you might need to add some water to keep it soupy.

This is great spooned over a thick slice of toasted bread with a sprinkling of walnut salsa (page 130).

MUSHY RICE

Dealing with mushy rice successfully is mostly in your head; mush is what you've got, and the sooner you slay your darling dreams of long and fluffy, united but joyfully independent grains of rice the better. Think instead of stewy comfort, and how what is lacking in texture you'll make up for with flavor.

Simplest scenario: You puree it with some or all of whatever you planned to eat with the rice (vegetable stir-fry, stew, beans, and so on) and, depending on what that was, add butter or oil, taste and adjust, seasoning with lemon or lime or vinegar, say, or soy sauce, hot sauce, fresh herbs, a sprinkle of ground spices, and so on, for a nice hearty soup. You might need to add some water if it's just too hearty.

Other options that pay off nicely with slightly more effort are:

- Stir an egg yolk, crumbled bacon, and plenty of black pepper into the hot mushy rice.
- Stir in plain yogurt and top with walnuts (see Tips, page 8) and maple syrup.
- Stir in shavings of katsuobushi (dried and smoked skipjack tuna), sliced scallions, and sesame oil. Sprinkle with sesame seeds and soy sauce.
- Stir in a lot of grated cheese and butter, a couple eggs, and a handful of sliced scallions and spread the mixture into a baking dish. Top with bread crumbs and bake at 375°F until hot and browned, about 20 minutes.

COCONUT RICE PUDDING WITH GINGER

Feel free to substitute other dried fruits for the raisins—mango, pineapple, dates, and so on—or to leave it smooth and skip the fruits and nuts altogether.

MAKES 4 TO 6 SERVINGS

2 cups overcooked rice

2 cups whole milk

One 13.5-ounce can unsweetened coconut milk

⅓ cup lightly packed brown sugar

¼ teaspoon fine sea salt or kosher salt (unless the overcooked rice is already salted)

½ teaspoon pure vanilla extract

½ inch of fresh ginger, grated (about 1 teaspoon)

¼ cup toasted, shredded, unsweetened coconut (optional)

¼ cup raisins (optional)

¼ cup toasted pistachios or other nuts (optional; see Tips, page 8)

In a medium saucepan, combine all the ingredients and bring to a simmer over medium-high heat, stirring occasionally. Reduce the heat to low and cook until the mixture is thick like pudding, about 20 minutes, stirring occasionally.

Eat hot or, my preference (when I'm not in a hurry), pour into a dish and refrigerate until chilled through.

MUSHY RICE PANCAKES

I am not a breakfast stack eater, but I *do* love savory pancakes. These are great with dollops of yogurt sauce (page 134) and any chutneys or pickles you might have on hand.

MAKES 12 THREE-INCH PANCAKES

2 cups overcooked rice

1½ cups flour (rice or all-purpose or a combination)

1 teaspoon baking soda

½ teaspoon fine sea salt or kosher salt (if needed)

2 teaspoons ground turmeric

2 teaspoons ground cumin (see Tips, page 8)

1 teaspoon sweet paprika

Crushed red pepper flakes to taste

Cooking oil, olive or vegetable (see Tips, page 7)

1 egg

4 scallions, green *and* white parts, thinly sliced

2 tablespoons chopped fresh cilantro leaves and stems

1 tablespoon chopped mango pickle (optional)

Plain whole-milk yogurt (optional)

Put a baking sheet in the oven and heat the oven to 200°F for keeping the pancakes warm as you cook them in batches.

Taste the rice for saltiness—often overcooked rice can be a little salty too. This will determine how much salt you add to the batter. In a medium bowl, stir together the rice, flour, baking soda, salt (if needed), turmeric, cumin, paprika, and red pepper flakes. Add ¼ cup oil and the egg, and stir in enough water to form a loose, pancake-batter-like consistency—the precise amount of water depends on how wet your rice is, but start with 1¼ cups and add more as needed. Stir in the scallions and cilantro, and the mango pickle if using.

Heat a large skillet (see Tips, page 6) over medium heat, add a tablespoon of cooking oil, and fry up a tester cake to taste and make any needed adjustments. Fry spoonfuls of the batter until the edges of the pancakes are brown and bubbles are forming in the centers, about 4 minutes. Use a spatula to turn them and fry the other side. Hold the finished pancakes in the oven while you fry the rest. Eat hot, with dollops of yogurt if you like.

HACKING PACKAGES

After days and nights of incredible labour
and fatigue, I succeeded in discovering the
cause of generation and life; nay, more,
I became myself capable of bestowing
animation upon lifeless matter.

—MARY SHELLEY, *FRANKENSTEIN*

Because package hacking happens when you're already too hungry, it pays to be prepared for it—like assembling an emergency kit for a natural disaster. Nobody wants it to come, but here it comes: Be ready to stitch some stuff together.

I won't provide a recipe for what has become the most common package meal, instant ramen/Cup-a-Soup, because so many already have—a lot of them more qualified ramen-hackers than I. But it's impossible for me to think about hacking packaged foods without thinking about the most accomplished hacker I know, a man I met while assisting at a series of cooking classes in San Quentin State Prison. Quentin Cooks is a program started by Lisa Dombroski and Helaine Melnitzer, steadfast and compassionate women working to improve the lives and lots of the men incarcerated at San Quentin. Lisa and Lainy created a mini cooking school within the huge cafeteria kitchen that processes the meals served to the eight hundred men of H Unit. A padlocked shipping container parked just outside the back door holds cookware for the classes—the kitchen itself is industrially outfitted, with cooking options limited to flame-free expanses of flat-top griddles, steam-jacketed kettles the size of bathtubs, and a walk-in convection oven. When the program is in session, Quentin Cooks provides an opportunity for men to learn some cooking skills and eat some good food (all ingredients are high-quality donations) while they talk about favorite meals, things they miss, and what they might cook together next week.

Of course, I learned a lot, as one does when teaching, and especially in such a singularly controlled setting. The food that was regularly churned out of the prison kitchen, the men told me, was awful, flavorless at best (hot sauce was in great demand). Many men talked about ways they'd found to "cook" within the strict parameters of what was allowed in the housing blocks—large dormitories consisting of stacked bunk beds in low-walled, doorless, two-man cells. There was zero privacy, with open showers and toilets, and cooking could only be done with an electric water kettle as a heat source.

One guy, I'll call him Luke, was a big man with menacing tattoos on his neck that he noticed me trying not to look at. "I'm getting those lasered off first thing when I get out," he told me. "That's not who I am anymore." Luke was a self-proclaimed hack-master and he, like a number of the men, bragged in particular about his skills making rice bowls. Luke's claim that they were legend seemed to be confirmed by nods around the kitchen, though they may have been here-he-goes-again nods. Arrangements were, amazingly, made for a group of us to meet at Luke's bunk the following week for a rice bowl lesson.

As we signed in the next week, I spied Luke's bunkie sitting at a small stainless-steel table in the tiny common area of the block, cutting summer sausages into dice with a plastic knife. He said he was prepping for Luke's big show. He was cutting the sausages here, he explained, the broken remains of several flimsy knives scattered around him, because he'd given Luke permission to use his bunk for a counter surface on which to assemble the rice bowls. They'd rolled back his sleeping pad and bedding so that there would be room for the sixteen bowls Luke was going to make: enough for the two of them, the Chef (me, gulp), and the folks recording and filming the demo. The rest were for Luke's friends in the block who had brought their own bowls for him to fill.

Before describing Luke's rice bowls, I want to be clear that I am not romanticizing this recipe or this situation—these were men incarcerated in a racist and cruel system, one that is unjust, unequal, and in desperate need of reform, if not abolition. These men's interest in cooking sprung in large part from an interest in eating, as it does for all of us, but I also saw how much they craved some flavor often denied to them and was impressed by how they found every possible way to get it. I don't think I would ever use Luke's exact recipe—maybe he never would again once free—but I include it for how it exposes issues around access and agency and the inextinguishable drive to gain control of them. I don't pretend to know what the experiences of Luke or the other incarcerated men I met in San Quentin are like. I can say that we did connect, in a small but real way, over food.

Luke had sourced ingredients from the prison store, stuff sent in through the mail, and the whole pieces of produce they sometimes got with their chow ration. He had two electric kettles going for hot water and was restaurant-line-cook-level organized. The bowls started with a half package of instant ramen, a handful of instant rice, a few chopped pickles, and a crumbling of Flamin' Hot Cheetos (FHC). Boiling water was added to plump the noodles and rice and stirred vigorously to dissolve the flavorings from the packets and the color from the FHC. Cooking done, Luke began the many-layered saucing and garnishing process, beginning with diced raw onions, garlic powder, and a complex special sauce he'd concocted with soy sauce, leftover pancake syrup, sriracha, and jelly. A sprinkling of the sausages that Bunkie had prepared was followed by a confident squirt of cheese. In an operation that I admit I did not fully understand, Bunkie held open a large plastic bag while Luke opened a package of pork rinds, threw in handfuls of them and more FHC, doused them both with special sauce and extra jolts of sriracha, and tossed them till they crackled. He quickly strew them atop the bowls. A squeeze of mayonnaise, a spoonful of garlicky sambal, and they were ready.

I took a bite, closely watched as I knew I would be. Luke's creation was bright red, salty, sweet, a week's worth of snacks in one mouthful. I took a second bite—the second bite is where your tell can show, but I had nothing to hide. I'd been umamied before, and in fancy places. I know how taste buds that have been on the bench all season are called in as starting players flag, and how by the time it's over, all the buds will be thirsty and in need of a good rest before the next game.

As Luke and the other guys from Quentin Cooks would probably be the first to tell you, it's better to not eat packaged foods at all. It was a big part of the reason they signed up for the program: to get their hands on some good fresh food. Still, there are times when, for a variety of reasons, dinner has to be quick, easy, and out of a box. This chapter aims to help make those times taste and feel better.

POPCORN

Popcorn was a family staple when I was growing up. We popped it with oil, or margarine, or sometimes bacon grease, in a pot with a lid on the stovetop. We shook nothing other than the blue cylinder of iodized salt on it and were perfectly happy for years, with Tupperware tumblers of Pepsi on ice and episodes of *All in the Family* and *The Jeffersons.* A well-intentioned Christmas gift to the family, an air popper, destroyed all that, as new technology can. Loud as a leaf blower, it spewed dry gusts of barren kernels from its thick plastic ductwork as bits of

chaff drifted around the kitchen. There was a tiny removable metal drawer for melting the butter that it was too late for. DOA. Even butter can't fix *everything*.

Then it got worse. Someone in a flavor lab somewhere hit on what they thought we wanted buttered popcorn to taste and, especially, smell like. They mixed up a big batch, smeared it into bags with popcorn kernels, and named it after the machine it had to be cooked in: microwave. The fact that it can be popped with literally the push of a button and doesn't require cleanup (though there is a nonreusable bag that must be tossed) most likely contributes more to microwave popcorn's success than the skill and accuracy of that flavor tech: There is something faintly nauseating about what is intended to be its irresistible aroma. It's *too* close, somehow: creepy, like taxidermy, or robots.

The upshot is that butter on popcorn is ruined for me (I won't even go into the awful "butter" squirted into movie theaters' buckets!). But popcorn I will tire of only when my teeth give out. A while back I began an informal search for the best kernels, finding solid contenders from sources as disparate as a local organic family farm and Orville Redenbacher's. In the end what turned out to make the difference between okay and superb popcorn was not the quality of the kernel but the quantity of the oil. You don't have to have written the gospel to want to preach it, so here's the truth as I learned it: pop in a pot on the stove and use a *lot* of oil. More oil, actually, than corn. At first, I measured ½ cup vegetable oil for ⅓ cup kernels, but now I just eyeball it so that the oil nearly covers the kernels. They pop up full and crisp and nicely oiled, and with very few unpopped duds at the bottom.

Struggling to decide what to put on popcorn is the kind of struggle you want to have. Kick and yell, go wild. Here are some combos in popular rotation at my house:

- Good olive oil and ground black pepper (and optional grated Pecorino Romano for that cacio e pepe vibe)
- Lots of nutritional yeast and Tajín seasoning powder
- A tablespoon of sesame oil added to the popping oil, and furikake (Japanese spice and seaweed/dried fish/egg blend) ground with salt in a mortar or spice grinder to sprinkle over

Some other topping ideas to play around with on movie night:

- Butter browned with a cracked whole garlic clove (which you can then discard)
- Ground spices like cumin, coriander (see Tips, page 8), turmeric, and chile powder, mixed with salt for ease of sprinkling
- Pimentón de la Vera (smoky paprika), mixed (sparingly) with salt for ease of sprinkling
- Dukkah (an Egyptian condiment made with ground nuts and spices), ground with salt for ease of sprinkling
- Coconut oil, amchur (sour mango powder), sweet or spicy chile powder, and salt
- Cashew salsa (page 134)

INSTANT SOUP, A LOVE STORY

In 1986 I found a sixth-floor walk-up to sublet in Alphabet City, a neighborhood in Manhattan's East Village. It was a shared one-bedroom, but my apartment mate, who held the lease, was rarely there; he had a girlfriend and stayed with her pretty much always.

Despite paying my rent on time, I came home one weekend to find a notice stuck to the door, and that was it, we were kicked out. Which was okay because by then, my best friend, Kath, who had a place uptown, and I had fallen in love.

But before the eviction and consummation, I had started cooking for myself and for Kath. I was not a professional cook yet, just an artist chasing a side interest, and at first, everything was based on Knorr powdered soup base. Leek was a favorite. I added frozen peas and fresh vegetables from Chinatown shops or corner bodegas, but was too afraid to cook rice, and stubbornly wouldn't make Minute Rice, as my mother always had, though I remembered it fondly. It wasn't until much later that I learned secrets about rice that gave me the confidence to cook it, so for now, we just ate soup.

Looking back, it had most likely been an apple-sweetened, cauliflower-enhanced vegetable soup with curry powder and peas that finally sparked something.

"I love this soup," Kath said, shimmying in her seat a little with pleasure. It was late on a cold night and the soup was comforting and hot, but even so, I knew the soup wasn't *that* good. I began to see that it was *me* she loved, and that she had for a while. Light dawns, they say back in Boston, on Marblehead.

The next day, we went to Queens for an art opening. On the long bus ride out, I wondered how long we'd been in love. Can it be a fall that undramatic? A natural force, like gravity? Or love like a maple, strong enough to build a house in, but who notices a tree *growing*? Rolling slowly through Queens streets lined by dead November grass and yellow and white plastic bags shifting in the bus exhaust, I felt a deepening vulnerability, my emotions coming to just below the skin, the way they hadn't since more maudlin younger years. I'd buttoned up some since then and perceived this resurfacing as a threat. At the same time, some of those buttons *had* gotten tight—it would be a relief to undo them.

The show of graduate paintings was rangy and interesting, all over the place. It seemed like sweet anarchy until the artists began to speak about their pieces and things ramped up to high-level artspeak. Legitimate views, identities, and theories around intent, process, and product—topics that normally engaged me—seemed false and frustratingly impotent. I was suddenly a nineteen-year-old rebel again and began thinking that someone should do something *real*. Even I didn't know what I meant. I was restless and petulant. I found Kath and, hoping to not sound as adolescently skittish and indignant as I felt, suggested we go.

The long bus ride back into Manhattan was crowded for a Sunday afternoon, something to do with the New York Marathon that morning, and we stood, swaying and holding straps. We all but coupled on that interborough ride, crushed by a crowd whose pressing bodies read as encouragement, bumping and grinding through the stops (it was a local), only our jeans and black sweaters keeping us apart, and those we shed, back at the walk-up, and then nothing kept us apart.

VEGETABLE SOUP WITH CAULIFLOWER, APPLE, PEAS, AND SPICES

Here are two versions: out of the packet for when they're saying "Curry up, we are so hungry!"; from scratch for when curry flavor can curry favor.

KNORR VERSION

MAKES 4 SERVINGS

One 1.4-ounce package Knorr leek recipe mix

2 cups bite-size pieces cauliflower

1 tart apple, cut into little pieces

¼ teaspoon fine sea salt or kosher salt

1 tablespoon curry powder (or a mixture of ground cumin, coriander, fennel [see Tips, page 8], turmeric, and sweet paprika)

1 cup peas, frozen or cooked fresh

In a large soup pot, combine 4 cups water, the soup mix, cauliflower, apple, salt, and curry powder. Bring to a boil over high heat, stirring occasionally. Reduce the heat to a simmer and cook until the cauliflower is tender, about 10 minutes. Stir in the peas to warm them up, taste, adjust, and serve. Spoon plain yogurt or one of the yogurt sauces (page 134) on top of your bowl.

SCRATCH VERSION

¼ cup cooking oil, olive or vegetable (see Tips, page 7)

1 medium yellow onion, thinly sliced

1 teaspoon fine sea salt or kosher salt

1 head of cauliflower, trimmed of brown parts, thinly sliced

1 tart apple, peeled, cored, and thinly sliced

1 tablespoon curry powder (or a mixture of ground cumin, coriander, fennel [see Tips, page 8], turmeric, and paprika)

Vinegar (white, red, or cider) or lemon (optional)

1 cup peas, frozen or cooked fresh

Heat a soup pot over high heat and add the oil, then the onion and salt. Stir, reduce the heat to medium-low, and cover the pot. Check and stir after a few minutes, letting the moisture collected on the lid drip back into the pot to keep things steamy. Reduce the heat further if there's any browning going on, and re-cover. Cook like this until the onion is very tender, about 15 minutes. Add the cauliflower, apple, curry powder, and enough water to cover the cauliflower by a ½ inch—you can always thin the soup later if it turns out too thick. Bring to a boil, reduce the heat to a simmer, and cook until the cauliflower is very tender, about 20 minutes—a piece of cauliflower should be easily squashed with a spoon.

For the creamiest results, spin the soup in a blender or with an immersion blender, being very careful so hot soup doesn't spew all over. You can also puree it in a food processor or even just stir it vigorously with a spoon or whisk. Taste and adjust for flavor, adding salt or a splash of vinegar or lemon, and for texture, adding more water if too thick. Add the peas to the pureed soup and reheat, if needed, before serving. Spoon plain yogurt or one of the yogurt sauces (page 134) on top of your bowl.

HACKARONI AND CHEESE

My childhood friend Wesley loved to eat apples. The guy would eat the whole damn apple, no nibbled core once the flesh was gone. To him, everything south of the stem was game: seeds, hard parts, all crunched on down. I was always more of a cheese guy myself, and as uncool as "teenage cheese guy" sounds, it's actually worse. I was a teenage cheese guy who dabbled in Velveeta but mostly stuck to the American single, the cheese-food named for the fate of the dorky guy who eats it. By the time I'd graduated to string cheese, Wes had developed a preference for McIntoshes. When kids started calling us Mac and Cheese, I, for one, took my habit underground.

Mac and cheese from the box can be pretty satisfying in times when you don't have the will to make it from scratch but you do have a teeny cheesy craving. Here are some of the hacks at our house—I'd love to hear about yours, so tag me @calpeternell when you post your hackages.

These recipes are for a 6-ounce box of mac and cheese and will make enough for you and your Wesley, unless you are as hungry as a sixteen-year-old, then for just you.

- **The Wesley:** In a large pot, boil the macaroni in salted water until it tastes cooked to you. Meanwhile, eat the core, the seeds, and half the flesh of an apple (preferably McIntosh) and cut the other half into little pieces. Drain the macaroni and leave it in the colander for a minute while you put the pot back on medium heat. Add

2 tablespoons butter, and when it melts and foams, add ¼ cup toasted, chopped walnuts (see Tips, page 8) or hazelnuts; a few roughly chopped sage leaves; and the apple bits. Let sizzle for a minute, then stir in ¼ cup milk, the macaroni, and the cheese powder.

- **Beef Jerky and Spinach:** In a large pot, boil the macaroni in salted water until it tastes cooked to you. Drain the macaroni, leaving it in the colander for a minute while you put the pot back on low heat. Add ¼ cup milk, 2 tablespoons butter, and 1 ounce (or more or less if you like) chopped beef jerky. When the butter melts, add the macaroni and stir in the cheese powder, a big handful of fresh baby spinach, and a pinch of salt.

- **Mac and Peas (and Bacon):** In a large pot, boil the macaroni in salted water until it tastes cooked to you. Meanwhile, cut a couple slices of bacon into little strips. Put a cup of frozen peas in a colander and then drain the macaroni, leaving mac and peas in the colander for a minute while you put the pot back on medium heat. Add the bacon strips to the pot and sizzle till they are how you like them. Leave the grease in with the bacon (or, if that makes you uneasy, get rid of the bacon grease and add 2 tablespoons butter instead), add ¼ cup milk, the macaroni and peas, and the packet of cheese powder. Grind in a lot of black pepper.

- **Corn, Cilantro, and Lime:** In a large pot, boil the macaroni in salted water. If you're using corn cut fresh off the cob (2 ears or about 1½ cups), add it to the water at the same time as the mac. If using canned (one 15-ounce can, drained) or frozen (1½ cups), drop it into the water a minute before the mac is done. When the mac tastes cooked to you, drain it, saving a cup of the water. Return the mac and corn to the pot and add ¼ cup cream, 2 tablespoons butter, the juice of a lime, a handful of chopped cilantro leaves and stems, a couple scallions thinly sliced, a little crushed red pepper flakes or chopped fresh jalapeño, and half the cheese powder (save the rest to shake over popcorn!). Stir in a little of the reserved water if needed to make it saucier.

- **Miso:** This one is especially loved by . . . some of us. Add corn, or peas, or both, using the method described above— the sweetness helps to balance the salty miso.

  In a large pot, boil the macaroni in salted water until it tastes cooked to you. Drain the macaroni (save a cup of the water), leaving it in the colander for a minute while you put the pot back on low heat. Add ¼ cup milk, 1 tablespoon butter, and 1½ tablespoons miso paste. Stir to dissolve the miso, then stir in a couple of sliced scallions, the macaroni, half the cheese powder (save the rest to shake over popcorn!), and 2 teaspoons sambal oelek or other chile paste (optional, but highly recommended!). Stir in a little of the reserved water if needed to make it saucier.

CAN OF BEANS: MASH-UP FRY-UPS, SALADS, AND SAUCES

Maybe I'm the only one who remembers when Robin Williams, at full boil, accepted the Oscar for *Good Will Hunting*, gushing, "I wanna thank the cast and crew, especially the people of South Boston: You're a can of corn, you're the best!" Surely, I am among the few who thought it my culinary duty to realize he meant they were great, easy, like a sweet fly ball falling right into your mitt (or, in the case of Southies, perhaps, right into your dumb mug). That's what a can of beans can be too, even more so. (See My Cakes: Nacho Cakes, page 67, for another tasty thing to do with a can of beans.)

Mash-up fry-ups: Mini recipes for when you don't want to do much more than open a can, but you do want to eat something tastier than that. Mash-up fry-ups are good straight or with rice and/or a couple of tortillas, on toast, on a bun (lightly spread with mayonnaise and mustard, with lettuce, tomato, a slice of onion, and pickles, and it's basically a bean smash burger).

Or, with a quick spin in the blender or food processor, MUFUs are easily convertible into dips or sauces (page 129) to spread on plates of salads, grilled or roasted vegetables, eggs, or meh meats.

THE MITTS-FULL MUFU: CAN OF CORN AND CAN OF BLACK BEANS

MAKES 2 PECKISH SERVINGS OR 1 HUNGRY SERVING

One 15-ounce can black beans

One 15-ounce can corn kernels

3 tablespoons cooking oil, olive or vegetable (see Tips, page 7)

2 scallions, green *and* white parts, thinly sliced

Fine sea salt or kosher salt

1 garlic clove, chopped

1 teaspoon whole cumin seeds (see Tips, page 8)

¼ teaspoon grated orange zest

Crushed red pepper flakes

½ cup roughly chopped fresh cilantro stems and leaves

Drain the black beans and corn, reserving their liquids. Set aside.

Heat a large skillet (see Tips, page 6) over medium heat and add the oil, then the scallions and ¼ teaspoon salt. Cook for 2 minutes, stirring occasionally. Add the garlic, cumin, zest, pepper flakes, and cilantro and stir for 30 seconds. Add the beans and corn and use a fork or the back of a spoon to mash them up a little as they fry. Add ¼ cup of the reserved liquid, ¼ teaspoon salt, bring to a simmer, taste, adjust, and eat hot.

WHITE BEAN MUFU: TUSCAN STYLE

MAKES 2 PECKISH SERVINGS OR 1 HUNGRY SERVING

One 15-ounce can white beans (cannellini, great northern, navy, or similar)

3 tablespoons cooking oil, olive or vegetable (see Tips, page 7)

1 garlic clove, chopped

½ teaspoon fennel seeds, crushed or ground (see Tips, page 8)

½ teaspoon chopped fresh rosemary leaves

1 tablespoon chopped fresh parsley leaves

Fine sea salt or kosher salt, plus more to taste

Ground black pepper

Good olive oil

Drain the beans, reserving the liquid. Set aside.

Heat a large skillet (see Tips, page 6) over medium heat. Add the oil and then the garlic, fennel seeds, rosemary, parsley, ¼ teaspoon salt, and pepper and stir for 30 seconds. Add the beans and use a fork or the back of a spoon to mash them up a little as they fry. Add ¼ cup of the reserved liquid, ¼ teaspoon salt, bring to a simmer, taste, adjust, and eat hot with tablespoons of good olive oil spooned over.

THE GARBONANZA MUFU: CHICKPEA WITH TURMERIC AND CILANTRO

MAKES 2 PECKISH SERVINGS OR 1 HUNGRY SERVING

One 15-ounce can chickpeas

3 tablespoons cooking oil, olive or vegetable (see Tips, page 7)

2 scallions, green *and* white parts, thinly sliced

Fine sea salt or kosher salt, plus more to taste

1 garlic clove, chopped

1 teaspoon ground turmeric

1 teaspoon coriander seeds, crushed or ground (see Tips, page 8)

Crushed red pepper flakes

½ cup roughly chopped fresh cilantro stems and leaves

1 lime, cut into wedges

1 or 2 eggs, hard-boiled, poached, or fried (optional)

Drain the chickpeas, reserving ¼ cup of the liquid. Set aside.

Heat a large skillet (see Tips, page 6) over medium heat and add the oil, then the scallions and ¼ teaspoon salt. Cook for 2 minutes, stirring occasionally. Add the garlic, turmeric, coriander, pepper flakes, and cilantro and stir for 30 seconds. Add the chickpeas and use a fork or the back of a spoon to mash them up a little as they fry. Add ¼ cup of the reserved liquid, ¼ teaspoon salt, bring to a simmer, taste, adjust, and eat hot with wedges of lime for squeezing, and an egg in each bowl, if you like.

RED BEAN MUFU: SMOKY STYLE

MAKES 2 PECKISH SERVINGS OR 1 HUNGRY SERVING

One 15-ounce can red beans

3 tablespoons cooking oil, olive or vegetable (see Tips, page 7)

2 scallions, green *and* white parts, thinly sliced

Fine sea salt or kosher salt, plus more to taste

1 garlic clove, chopped

½ chipotle chile or ¼ teaspoon pimentón de la Vera (smoked paprika)

½ teaspoon paprika

1 teaspoon chopped fresh thyme leaves or ¼ teaspoon dried

1 tablespoon chopped fresh parsley leaves

Generous grindings of black pepper

Drain the beans, reserving the liquid. Set aside.

Heat a large skillet (see Tips, page 6) over medium heat and add the oil, then the scallions and ¼ teaspoon salt. Cook for 2 minutes, stirring occasionally. Add the garlic, chipotle, paprika, thyme, parsley, and black pepper and stir for 30 seconds. Add the beans and use a fork or the back of a spoon to mash them up a little as they fry. Add ¼ cup of the reserved liquid, ¼ teaspoon salt, bring to a simmer, taste, adjust, and eat hot.

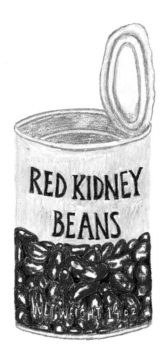

CANNELLINI BEAN AND CELERY SALAD WITH ANCHOVIES

A quick, stylish salad to throw together and eat as an appetizer or an easy lunch. The celery is raw for extra crunch with the soft beans.

MAKES 4 SERVINGS

One 15-ounce can white beans (cannellini, Great Northern, navy, or similar)

¼ cup plus 1 tablespoon good olive oil

1 small garlic clove, grated or pounded to a paste (see Tips, page 7)

Fine sea salt or kosher salt, plus more to taste

3 or 4 celery stalks, thinly sliced on an angle for the swoosh

½ cup fresh parsley leaves, whole if tender-ish, chopped if not

Juice from ½ lemon

Ground black pepper

One 4-ounce can anchovy fillets, drained and sliced in half lengthwise

Drain the white beans really well and reserve the liquid. Put the beans in a blender or food processor with ¼ cup of the olive oil, the garlic, and ¼ teaspoon salt and spin smooth. If needed, add just enough of the reserved liquid to make pureeing happen—too much liquid will make the beans taste washed out. Spread the bean mash on a platter.

In a large bowl, combine the celery, parsley, 1 tablespoon olive oil, the lemon juice, a sprinkle of salt, and a grind of black pepper. Toss to coat well, taste, adjust, and scatter over the beans. Adorn with the strips of anchovies.

Variation

Make a salad into a sandwich (often a good instinct) by spreading the bean stuff onto slices of bread and pile on the celery salad and anchovies. Or do the same with toasts and leave open-faced to have as an appetizer. For both variations, you may want to quickly boil the celery (see page 90) to take the edge off the crunch.

CAN OF BEANS COOKED WITH RICE AND LOTS OF SCALLIONS AND CILANTRO

This is what I make after hours, home from the club with new friends, boa off and flame up. Actually, it's what I make for lunch when I'm still in my sweats, forgot to eat breakfast, and am ready to chew open a can of beans. Deliciously restores you to full club strength.

MAKES ENOUGH FOR THREE CLUB KIDS OR ONE REALLY HUNGRY KID

¼ cup cooking oil, olive or vegetable (see Tips, page 7)

1 bunch of scallions, green *and* white parts, thinly sliced

½ bunch of fresh cilantro, stems and leaves roughly chopped

1 garlic clove, unpeeled, cracked

1 teaspoon fine sea salt or kosher salt

1 cup long-grain white rice

One 15-ounce can brown beans (or black, red, or white beans)

Heat a large skillet (see Tips, page 6) over medium heat and add the oil, then the scallions, cilantro, garlic, and salt. Cook for 1 minute, stirring occasionally, then add the rice, beans and their liquid, and 1 cup water. Bring to a simmer, stirring occasionally, reduce the heat to low, cover, and cook until the rice is done, about 15 minutes. Add a little water and continue cooking if the rice seems undone but the skillet is drying out. Let sit for 5 minutes off the heat if you can stand it before eating.

Variation with Eggs

Just before covering, use a spoon to make two divots in the rice and crack an egg into each. Sprinkle the eggs with salt and proceed. This timing will result in eggs completely cooked through—if softer yolks are something you're looking for, wait to add the eggs until there are 8 minutes left in the cooking time.

CHICKPEAS WITH TOMATO, ROSEMARY, AND CREAM

Doesn't need to be pasta sauce, but *is* a great pasta sauce. Also works with toasts, rice, salad . . .

MAKES 2 TO 4 SERVINGS, DEPENDING ON ACCOMPANIMENTS

¼ cup cooking oil, olive or vegetable (see Tips, page 7)

1 smallish red onion, diced or thinly sliced

½ teaspoon fine sea salt or kosher salt

1 garlic clove, chopped

1 teaspoon chopped fresh rosemary leaves

Crushed red pepper flakes

Half a 15-ounce can tomatoes (about 1 cup), chopped fine, with their juices

One 15-ounce can chickpeas, drained, liquid reserved

½ cup light or heavy cream (but not half-and-half; it will break)

2 tablespoons chopped fresh parsley leaves

Chopped anchovy fillets or crumbled canned sardines (to taste, and only if you want)

Heat a skillet (see Tips, page 6) over high heat, add the oil, then add the onion and salt. Stir until things get sizzling, then reduce the heat to medium and cook, stirring occasionally, until the onion is soft but not browned, about 15 minutes. Add the garlic, rosemary, and red pepper flakes and stir for 30 seconds. Add the tomatoes and reduce the heat to a slow simmer, letting the mixture bubble amiably for 5 minutes or so, stirring occasionally. Add the chickpeas, cream, and parsley and bring back to a simmer. The texture can be thickened by further simmering or thinned by adding the reserved chickpea liquid. If you are using anchovies or sardines, stir them in.

SARDINE AND ANCHOVY S'COOL

Tuna's not cool—I gave it up years ago. You can easily look up the reasons why; for your health and the health of the fishery, you should probably do it too, but wait! Let me give you the good news first (with supporting recipes in case you are unable to take my word for it that this constitutes good news): Sardines and anchovies are totally cool to eat! Though some like to eat anchovy fillets straight, especially with bread or radishes and butter, they are most useful as a flavor-packed ingredient. Sardines, on the other fin, are popularly eaten right from the tin with toasts or crackers. My dad used to enjoy temporary pariah status eating sardines alone with mustard, raw onions, and a beer, and I do too, particularly when I'm feeling maudlin and want to pretend I am broke, or heartbroken, or breaking into the emergency rations during a zombie attack.

When I'm feeling less sorry for myself, I make one of these two recipes to slurp with friends.

SPAGHETTI WITH CREAM, GARLIC, AND ANCHOVIES

I love anchovies so much I wrote a book about them! Well, a third of a book (*Almonds, Anchovies, and Pancetta*). So this super-easy and quick recipe from the beloved mentor I wish I had met, Marcella Hazan, came as a welcome surprise. I've adapted it here using anchovies instead of tuna. I won't sin and say it's better. But you could.

MAKES 4 SERVINGS

Fine sea salt or kosher salt

1 pound spaghetti

1 egg

1 small garlic clove, grated or pounded to a paste (see Tips, page 7)

One 2-ounce can anchovy fillets, drained and finely chopped or pounded with the garlic

3 tablespoons butter

⅔ cup light or heavy cream (but not half-and-half; it will break)

½ cup grated Parmesan or Grana Padano cheese

2 tablespoons chopped fresh parsley leaves

Ground black pepper and/or crushed red pepper flakes

Put a big pot of cold water on to boil. Add salt and the spaghetti and cook, stirring occasionally, until it's the way you like it, 10 to 12 minutes.

Meanwhile, in the large bowl you intend to serve the pasta in, whisk the egg until no longer streaky and then mix in the garlic, anchovies, butter, cream, cheese, parsley, ¼ teaspoon salt, and grindings of black pepper or red pepper flakes or both.

Drain the spaghetti when done, reserving ½ cup of the water. Stir half the reserved water into the cream mixture to warm it up, then stir in the spaghetti. Taste and adjust, adding a pinch more of salt or cheese and getting the texture right with more pasta water as needed.

PASTA WITH SARDINES

This tinned take on a Sicilian classic brings in enough flavors—aromatic saffron and fennel, sweet raisins, toasty almonds—to win over the sardine reluctant.

MAKES 4 SERVINGS

Fine sea salt or kosher salt

Olive oil

1 yellow onion, diced

1 small fennel head, diced

Pinch of saffron threads, crushed to powder with the back of a spoon

1 pound bucatini or spaghetti

1 or 2 garlic cloves, chopped

Crushed red pepper flakes to taste

1 teaspoon fennel seeds, ground (see Tips, page 8)

One 4-ounce can sardines, drained

¼ cup raisins, soaked in hot water to plump, then drained

¼ cup toasted almonds (see Tips, page 8), chopped

1 teaspoon chopped fresh oregano or marjoram—dried works too (optional)

2 tablespoons chopped fresh parsley leaves

Put a big pot of cold water on to boil. Add salt.

Heat a large skillet (see Tips, page 6) over high heat and add 3 tablespoons olive oil, then the onion, fennel, saffron, and a light sprinkle of salt. Stir the onion until sizzling, then turn to medium and cook, stirring occasionally, until soft but not browned, about 15 minutes.

Put the pasta in the pot of boiling water and stir occasionally while you finish the sauce.

Move the onion and fennel to the perimeter of the skillet and add the garlic, red pepper flakes, and fennel seeds to center stage, adding oil if it's dry there. When the garlic is just right, after about 30 seconds, add the sardines, raisins, almonds, and herbs. Stir, adding a splash of water if needed for flow.

Drain the pasta when it tastes done, after 10 to 12 minutes, reserving ½ cup of the water. Mix the pasta into the sauce, taste and adjust for salt and oiliness, adding pasta water as needed to get the texture right.

HAMBURG-A-RONI: CAMPFIRE EDITION

When I first made this while we were sheltering in place together last year, my eldest got kind of mad at me. You wouldn't really make this, they said, their tone a mixture of wary challenge and slight betrayal. They weren't wrong; I wouldn't make this. Or rather, I'd do it a different way, the longer way that doesn't include shortcuts and is, with plenty of time, skills, and long simmering, more deeply, naturally flavorful. I was on the verge of cutting Hamburg-A-Roni and, indeed, this whole chapter from my table of contents when I realized that they weren't quite right either: At a one-pot cookout, like while camping, I *would* make this. Also, I liked that the technique for cooking the unboiled pasta directly in the sauce is the same one used for classy Spanish fideus. I decided to double down on the campy, adding chipotle chiles to help evoke campfire shadows and smoke. The rib-sticking beef, cheese, and butter combination tucks you, warm and round, into your sleeping bag. Maybe skip the s'mores tonight.

MAKES 4 SERVINGS

1 pound ground beef (grass-fed, if possible; see Tips, page 10)

2½ teaspoons fine sea salt or kosher salt

Ground black pepper

2 tablespoons cooking oil, olive or vegetable (see Tips, page 7), or butter

1 medium yellow onion, diced

2 garlic cloves, minced

1 chipotle chile in adobo sauce (or more, you spicy!), or crushed red pepper flakes to taste

Pinch of dried oregano

One 15-ounce can whole peeled tomatoes with their juices, chopped

1 pound dry pasta (if using spaghetti, break them in half *great sound*)

One 15-ounce can corn kernels (optional, extra campy), with liquid

6 cups hot water—boiling is good, hot tap is fine

1 cup grated Cheddar cheese (from 2 ounces)

3 tablespoons butter

Break up the ground beef on a plate and sprinkle with 1 teaspoon of the salt and the black pepper to taste.

Heat a pot or pan big enough to hold the pasta once cooked over medium-high heat, add the oil, then the beef right away. Poke the beef to spread it out, spread the onion over it, then leave everything alone to brown. Stir when the meat gets some good color, about 5 minutes, and let the other sides brown, about 3 minutes more. Add the garlic, chipotle,

(continued)

and oregano and stir for 30 seconds. Add the tomatoes and their juices, increase the heat to high, and cook, stirring occasionally, for 3 minutes. Add the uncooked pasta, the corn and its liquid (if using), 5½ cups of the water, and the remaining 1½ teaspoons of salt. Bring to a boil, stirring often, then lower to a simmer. Continue stirring occasionally, adding water as needed to keep things wet while the pasta cooks.

Taste a piece to determine doneness and, when it's how you like it, add any salt it may need and the cheese and butter, stirring well until melted. Eat on plates or from bowls, or just squat around the pot camp-style.

Variation

Skip the pasta and add a can or two of black or other beans and you've got chili!

EGGS

The original packaged food is the egg, and that, as they say in France, is really enough. (Sorry, and props to Mr. Tanis.) As far as putting lipstick on an egg, the easiest way, and perhaps best way, is to cook it, in its packaging, in boiling water for 8 or 9 minutes, peel it, cut it in half, and sprinkle with salt and crushed sweet red chiles like Marash, Aleppo, or smoky Urfa—all credible lipstick hue names. (Lipstick companies: I'd consider sponsorship opportunities if you need me.) Mmwah!

TORTILLA ESPAÑOLA ON VACATION

With vacation comes relaxation, and with relaxation comes inspiration. French fries help too. I was working through an XXL pile of them at a roadside diner on my way to a few days of vacation, and I finally cried uncle. But there was still an XL pile left, and that's when tortilla española revealed itself as the perfect lipstick-on-an-egg-with-leftover-fries-on-vacation dish! Sure, you could finish the tortilla by painting on salsa-red lips if you want.

MAKES 6 SERVINGS

3 tablespoons cooking oil, olive or vegetable (see Tips, page 7), plus more as needed

Enough leftover French fries to mostly fill your non-stickiest skillet

6 eggs

1 teaspoon fine sea salt or kosher salt

Ground black pepper

4 scallions, green *and* white parts, thinly sliced

Heat a skillet (see Tips, page 6) over medium heat and add 1 tablespoon of the oil and the French fries. Let them crisp and brown a little, stirring occasionally, for 3 to 4 minutes. Meanwhile, crack the eggs into a medium bowl, add the salt, some black pepper, and the remaining 2 tablespoons oil, and whisk until uniformly yellow with no streaks.

Reduce the heat to low and add the scallions to the skillet. Cook for 2 to 3 minutes, then pour in the eggs, tilting the skillet to fill in any gaps. Keep the heat low and rotate the skillet occasionally to encourage even cooking. When the edges of the tortilla look set and the center is still somewhat liquid, about 8 minutes, run a knife around the sides of the skillet and carefully slide a metal spatula under the tortilla to loosen the underside. Tilt the skillet and use the spatula to encourage the tortilla to slide out onto a plate, uncooked side up.

Make sure that the skillet still has a coating of oil, then invert it over the tortilla. Using hot pads, put one hand under the plate and the other atop the inverted skillet. Now the exciting part: flip the tortilla back into the skillet. The motion should be up and over, not just over, and it has to happen kind of quickly. Don't worry if things are looking a little Humpty Dumpty; just fit it all back together again and continue cooking over low heat.

When it's cooked through—about another 8 minutes, but make a crack in the middle and sneak a peek to make sure—slide the tortilla out onto a plate. Or flip it onto a plate if you think the other side looks better. A tortilla improves after it cools, at least a little.

Cut in wedges or squares and serve with the leftover packet of ketchup that came with the fries, or with Ranch Dressing (page 71) or Red Bean MUFU sauce (page 50).

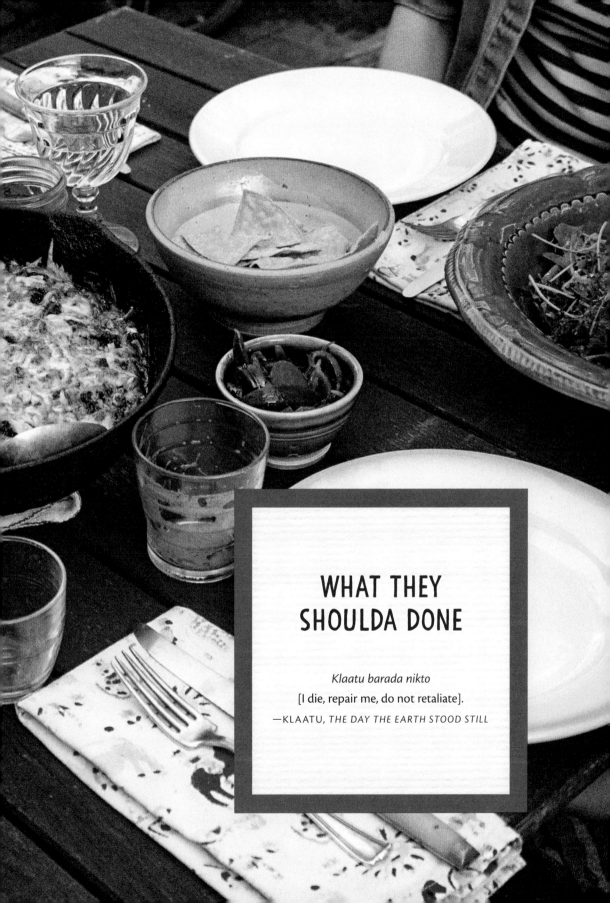

WHAT THEY
SHOULDA DONE

Klaatu barada nikto
[I die, repair me, do not retaliate].
—KLAATU, *THE DAY THE EARTH STOOD STILL*

I'm a fan of sci-fi movies. I like taking little tours around space and time and entering alternate realities that enable me to see our own with new clarity. Restaurants are like sci-fi, each big-banging out their own universe, cooking up their swirling world of dishes. Chefs are confident that their versions are the best, the real thing, and are sometimes willing to Death Star any who dare deny it. As an eater, though, I say bring on the variations, and if they are dead, repair them with empathy. If you can't locate your favorite among the stars, create your own. Isn't defining authenticity all but impossible anyway, and declaring it, foolish?

Take Caesar salad. For the longest time I was outraged that it should ever be made without anchovies: There was not a slender fillet of doubt in my mind that salty little fishes were the very soul of the classic salad. Surprise: The original Caesar Cardini version

did not include them! Unless it did—some say it was Alessandro Cardini, Caesar's brother, whose anchovy-spiked dressing made the salad what it is today. Either way, the scales have fallen from my eyes and I feel, not unpleasantly, adrift.

Still, how *did* bright orange liquid cheese become the default for nachos? Why *should* chowder be so thick that a spoon stands in it? Why *must* ranch dressing be so sweet you wonder if they dressed your salad with a milkshake by mistake? We're not going to find a single answer that's right for everyone—that doesn't exist. But each of us can find out for ourselves on a journey that is the destination.

I'm not doing any straight-setting of the record here—let the record remain gloriously bent, I say—but I have been dispirited by some restaurant versions of otherwise perfectly good classics, and, in fondness and support, I offer here my universions.

NACHOS, TWO WAYS

We burned through many bags of tortilla chips and a couple of toaster ovens bringing up our three sons. I never showed them how to make nachos, because who needs instructions for how to sprinkle beans and cheese onto chips? Well, these two versions take nachos up a notch (oh, forgive me!), and won't catch your toaster oven on fire.

NACHOS WITH QUESO FUNDIDO (MOLTEN CHEESE)

You'll never look back to pumpable orange stadium goo once you dig into the greasy-good realness of this queso fundido. Roll stringy spoonfuls into warm tortillas with something to counter the fat, like the fresh or pickled crunchy accompaniments below.

MAKES 4 TO 6 SERVINGS

1 pound Mexican chorizo sausage, removed from the casings and crumbled

1 tablespoon cooking oil, olive or vegetable (see Tips, page 7)

1 yellow or white onion, diced

Fine sea salt or kosher salt

8 ounces low-moisture, whole-milk mozzarella, grated

4 ounces Cheddar cheese, grated

Flour or corn tortillas or tortilla chips (optional)

Lettuce and/or arugula leaves or shredded cabbage (optional)

Pickled onions, carrots, or jalapeños (optional)

Scallions, green *and* white parts, thinly sliced (optional)

Cilantro sprigs, whole or roughly chopped (optional)

Heat the oven to 450°F.

Heat a large skillet (see Tips, page 6) over medium-high heat and add the oil, then the chorizo. Allow the chorizo to brown on one side, about 5 minutes, then add the onion and ¼ teaspoon salt and stir. Cook, stirring occasionally, until the chorizo is done and the onion is tender, about another 8 minutes. Tip the mixture out onto a plate and if there is simply too much grease, tilt the plate and spoon some of it away (see Tips, page 11).

Mix the cheeses together. If your skillet is oven-safe, spread half of the cheese mixture over the bottom, or use a baking dish, preferably one that's deep but not too big, so that the queso fundido isn't spread too thin. Top with the chorizo-onion mixture and the remaining cheese and bake until melted and bubbly, 15 to 20 minutes. Eat with some or all of the optional ingredients.

Vegetarian Variation

Replace the chorizo with romesco sauce. To make romesco, mix toasted bread crumbs with chopped toasted nuts (almonds, walnuts, and/or hazelnuts), chili paste that's not too spicy, garlic paste (see Tips, page 7), a splash of red wine vinegar or sherry vinegar, and enough olive oil to make it a thick paste.

MY CAKES, NACHO CAKES

When you get to the end of the bag of tortilla chips and all you have left are pieces too small for salsa-dipping, make these pan-fried patties. The smushed beans join with the broken chips to form a proto-batter that just barely—gently, let's say—holds things together while the melting cheese gets a little crispy-burnt around the edges.

MAKES 4 SERVINGS

2 cups broken tortilla chips

One 15-ounce can pinto beans, drained, liquid discarded

3 ounces grated Cheddar or Jack cheese

2 scallions, green *and* white parts, thinly sliced

¼ cup roughly chopped fresh cilantro leaves and tender stems

1½ teaspoons toasted whole cumin seeds or ½ teaspoon ground cumin (see Tips, page 8)

Crushed red pepper flakes

¼ teaspoon fine sea salt or kosher salt

2 tablespoons cooking oil, olive or vegetable (see Tips, page 7), plus more for frying

Favorite hot sauce

1 lime, cut into quarters

In a large bowl, combine the chips, beans, cheese, scallions, cilantro, cumin, red pepper flakes, salt, and oil. Using your hands, mix very well, squeezing the mixture between your fingers to break up the beans and chips until the mixture begins to hold together. It will still be pretty crumbly, but don't worry; the pieces that fall away in the skillet become tasty, crispy snacklets.

Heat a large skillet (see Tips, page 6) over medium heat. Add a couple tablespoons of oil and place little piles of the mixture in the skillet, spreading them out flat with your fingers or pressing with a spatula. Cook until they are browning around the edges, about 4 minutes, then flip them over to brown the other side, about 4 minutes.

Remove to a plate and eat right away or keep warm in the oven while you fry the rest. Dashes of hot sauce, a squeeze of lime? Yes please.

MILO'S BEAN DIP

Arriving home hungry after high school, my son Milo would eat straight-up slices of cheese doused with hot sauce. This was difficult for me to watch—the gory red splatters of Crystal making a desperate snack seem almost criminal. I risked/guaranteed being annoying with a series of "Wouldn't you like some _____ with that?" questions until he finally not only gave in but nailed it with this bean dip recipe that still retains a heart of hot sauce and block cheese.

FEEDS 1. ALL INGREDIENT QUANTITIES ARE "SOME."

Cooking oil, olive or vegetable (see Tips, page 7)

Red, yellow, or white onions or scallions, sliced or diced

Fine sea salt or kosher salt

Cumin, raw or toasted, whole or ground (see Tips, page 8)

A can of beans—black, pinto, or refried

Cheddar or Jack cheese

Hot sauce

Cilantro sprigs, chopped

Heat a large skillet (see Tips, page 6) over medium heat. Add a couple tablespoons of oil, then cook the onions with salt until wilted and turning transparent, about 5 minutes. Or don't cook them. In any case, combine all the ingredients in a skillet and bring to magma eruption over heat as aggressive as your appetite + timeline. Burn your mouth, or "let the dip cool" while you change into your play clothes.

DRESSINGS

"What kind of pajamas do you wear?" I heard my son Milo ask the cowboy as they passed above me on a switchback. "Mine are Spider-Man."

We were riding horses through the rugged and gorgeous desert outside Tucson. Milo was four and hadn't stopped talking since Lucky, his favorite cowboy, had set him atop the fastest horse in the stable, whose full name was Jetlag but to Milo he was just Jet. Long-suffering leather-faced Lucky had been grunting a string of yeps to the boy's bottomless curiosity but couldn't seem to muster one now. Either he was stumped by the pajamas question, or they had just moved out of earshot. At the next switchback, Milo looked down at me and yelled across the spiky barrels and waving saguaros, "Dad! Lucky doesn't wear *any* pajamas!"

Back at the dude ranch, Milo succumbed to the pull of the cacti, and there was just enough time before dinner for the Elmer's glue we'd painted on his prickled palms to dry and peel off. The dining room was all wagon-wheel fixtures, saddle blankets, and laminated maps. Tables set with bandanna napkins, pebbled plastic tumblers of iced tea, and there, at the end of the salad bar, the inevitable: ranch. It was a dressing I'd scorned, but now I saw that the chopped iceberg, cold garbanzos, and not-sliced-today cucumbers were going to require something drastic. There was Caesar too, and I had the ladle halfway to my bowl when I noticed my wife furiously shaking her head at me. She had been betrayed by Caesar, and I, not one to ignore a warning, reversed course and dipped into the ranch instead. Soon, I found that almost everything at the Lazy K was improved with the stuff. I felt guilty: I'll only eat ranch at a ranch, I reasoned, detecting the dill, savoring the slight sourness, knowing I was lying to myself.

Simple vinaigrettes are great when what they are dressing is too; other times, there's ranch (and a proper Caesar). Also figgy (page 22), ginger-lime (page 20), peanut-ginger (page 90), and yogurt sauces (page 134).

RANCH DRESSING

No one needs to be told what to do with ranch dressing, but there's raw egg in it, if you need to be told that.

¼ cup plain whole-milk yogurt

1 egg yolk

Juice of half a lemon

1 garlic clove

2 tablespoons roughly chopped chives or scallions, green *and* white parts

2 tablespoons roughly chopped fresh dill leaves and tender stems (from 3 or 4 sprigs)

1 tablespoon roughly chopped fresh parsley leaves (from 3 or 4 sprigs)

½ cup cooking oil, olive or vegetable (see Tips, page 7)

A dash of Crystal hot sauce or other hot sauce

¼ teaspoon fine sea salt or kosher salt

Ground black pepper

Combine all the ingredients in a blender and whiz until smooth. Taste and correct for salt, lemon, spiciness, and so on.

Use right away or refrigerate for later. Keeps for a couple days.

CAESAR SALAD DRESSING

The making of Caesar salad dressing seems to invite wild experimentation leading to tragic consequences and widespread confusion. Ill-defined techniques and inappropriate toss-ins posed as inherited secret ingredients . . . forget all that. The piquant truth is that Caesar dressing is garlic and anchovy mayonnaise with cheese. Deal with the deliciousness.

MAKES A GENEROUS ½ CUP

1 small garlic clove, grated or pounded to a paste (see Tips, page 7)

6 anchovy fillets (half of a 2-ounce can or jar)

1 teaspoon Dijon mustard

1 teaspoon lemon juice

1 tablespoon red wine vinegar

Ground black pepper

¼ cup grated Parmesan or Grana Padano cheese

1 raw egg yolk (or 1 whole egg, boiled for 8 minutes and chopped, if more comfortable for you)

6 tablespoons olive oil

Mash the garlic and anchovies together, either in a mortar with the pestle or on a cutting board with a knife. Add the mustard, lemon juice, vinegar, pepper, and cheese to the mortar (or place them in a bowl with the garlic and anchovies) and stir to mix well. Add the egg yolk, then pour the olive oil in a thin stream as you stir spiritedly with the pestle or a whisk to form a thick emulsion. If it gets very thick and chunky looking, add a teaspoon of water or two to thin it back to creaminess. Taste and adjust for salt, lemon, cheese, and so on.

Use right away or refrigerate for later. Keeps for a day.

NOT-PESTOS

I love classic, capital-P Pesto—basil, pine nuts, cheese, garlic, oil, salt—so simple, but making it is kind of hard to get right. I've made it countless times and I am sure, by Genovese standards, every one of them has been a failure. Not, they might rule, even Pesto, really. And I am a chef! Imagine what they might say about all the processed iterations smeared across America. But hey, fine, if not-Pesto is what I make, I embrace my destiny, blender whirling and feeling freed from basil's browning and pine nuts' problems (see my book *Almonds, Anchovies, and Pancetta*). Maybe we'll meet again in Genoa.

Meanwhile, these pestos all do what Pesto does as a sauce for pasta and all the other things you want to put delicious green sauce on.

Pasta tip: Leave the remains of the pesto in the blender jar (it is impossible to get it all out, right?), then rinse with a little of the hot pasta water and use the resulting green slurry to get the texture of the finished dish right.

MARJORAM WALNUT NOT-PESTO

MAKES ABOUT 1½ CUPS

1 garlic glove

½ cup walnuts, toasted (see Tips, page 8) and skins rubbed off

½ cup olive oil, plus more as needed

1 small bunch of fresh marjoram, leaves picked from stems

1 big bunch of fresh Italian parsley, stems and leaves roughly chopped

1 cup grated Parmesan or Grana Padano cheese

½ teaspoon fine sea salt or kosher salt

In the jar of a blender, combine the garlic, walnuts, and olive oil and whiz till smooth. Add the remaining ingredients (marjoram can vary in its flavor and aromatic strength—you may want to hold some back) and whiz till smooth again, stopping two or three times to scrape the sides of the blender and push everything down, and adding more oil if needed. Taste and adjust.

Use right away or refrigerate for later. Keeps for a couple days.

ARUGULA ALMOND NOT-PESTO

MAKES ABOUT 1½ CUPS

1 garlic clove

½ cup almonds, toasted (see Tips, page 8) and skins rubbed off

½ cup olive oil, plus more as needed

3 ounces arugula, rinsed and dried (3 packed cups)

1 cup grated Parmesan or Grana Padano cheese

½ teaspoon fine sea salt or kosher salt

In the jar of a blender, combine the garlic, almonds, and olive oil and whiz till smooth. Add the remaining ingredients and whiz till smooth again, stopping two or three times to scrape the sides of the blender and push everything down, and adding more oil if needed. Taste and adjust.

Use right away or refrigerate for later. Keeps for a couple days.

CILANTRO PEANUT NOT-PESTO

MAKES ABOUT 1½ CUPS

1 garlic clove

1 inch of fresh ginger, thinly sliced across the grain (about 1 tablespoon)

Jalapeño pepper, seeded or not depending on how spicy you like it (optional)

½ cup roasted peanuts (see Tips, page 8)

½ cup vegetable oil, plus more as needed

1 big bunch of fresh cilantro, stems and leaves roughly chopped

½ cup coconut milk

½ teaspoon fine sea salt or kosher salt

Juice of 1 lime

In the jar of a blender, combine the garlic, ginger, jalapeño (if using), peanuts, and oil and whiz till smooth. Add the remaining ingredients and whiz till smooth again, stopping two or three times to scrape the sides of the blender and push everything down, and adding more oil if needed. Taste and adjust.

Use right away or refrigerate for later. Keeps for a couple days.

MINT PISTACHIO NOT-PESTO

MAKES ABOUT 1½ CUPS

1 garlic clove

½ cup toasted pistachios (see Tips, page 8)

½ cup olive oil, plus more as needed

1 bunch of mint, leaves picked from stems

½ bunch of Italian parsley, leaves and stems roughly chopped

1 cup grated Parmesan or Grana Padano cheese

½ teaspoon fine sea salt or kosher salt

In the jar of a blender, combine the garlic, pistachios, and olive oil and whiz till smooth. Add the remaining ingredients and whiz till smooth again, stopping two or three times to scrape the sides of the blender and push everything down, and adding more oil if needed. Taste and adjust.

Use right away or refrigerate for later. Keeps for a couple days.

UNTHICK CLAM CHOWDER:
NEW ENGLAND VERSION, DINER EDITION

No soup should be as thick as chowder so often is; soup spoons should be at rest, not standing like abandoned pier supports, tilting in the ebbing, sludgy tide. For me, the best chowder is briny, milky, and slightly sweet with corn, chewy with clams, smoky with bacon. Happily, this unthickness is not hard to achieve, but to make it easier, let's try a little role-playing: You're a short-order cook in a beachside town. You start the morning by laying out the bacon and spreading potatoes and onions across the flattop. It's 5 a.m., still dark, too early to even gauge whether you're hungover or not. It's a weekday, which precludes nothing—you're partying every night because it's your summer job and the beach is *right there*, all warm night long. You're drinking black coffee because just looking at the carton of cream gave you a belly-flop so maybe you *are* hungover or maybe you're saving the cream for the chowder lunch special. Could be both. Dozens of any-style eggs later, you gather the leftover home fries and bacon into a soup pot, crank open cans of clams and corn, and find your courage with the cream. The incoming lunch cook tries it and smiles, so you untie your apron and take the stool at the end of the counter with a restorative bowl, the sandy grit in your board shorts serving as last night's grinding reminder and tonight's shimmering promise.

MAKES 3 SERVINGS

2 tablespoons butter

½ medium yellow onion, diced

2 bacon slices, cut across into thin strips

1 tennis ball–size yellow potato (Yukon Gold, Yellow Finn, or similar), cut into ½-inch dice

Fine sea salt or kosher salt

1 teaspoon chopped thyme leaves (3 to 4 sprigs' worth; optional)

1 bay leaf

Ground black pepper

One 6½-ounce can clams with liquid

One 11-ounce can corn kernels with liquid

¼ cup cream

2 tablespoons chopped fresh parsley leaves (from about 6 sprigs)

Heat a large skillet (see Tips, page 6) over medium heat. Add the butter and when it melts, the onion, bacon, potato, and ¼ teaspoon salt. Stir until things get sizzling, then reduce the heat to medium-low, cover, and cook, stirring occasionally, for 10 minutes. Add the thyme and bay leaf, grind in black pepper, and stir for half a minute.

Add the clams and corn with their juices, the cream, and ½ cup water and increase the heat to bring to a simmer. When the potatoes are cooked through, about 5 minutes, stir in the parsley, taste, adjust, and serve.

SCHMEGETABLES

We're all born naked and the rest is drag.

—RUPAUL

Eating even perfect vegetables naked can get boring. It's okay to want to dress up a little, for flavor, for presentation, maybe just for kicks and glitter. This is especially true when the vegetables are just so-so. They often are lacking sweetness, texture, and robust flavor, so I try to brighten those qualities in a couple of different ways.

In the alternative world where I am vegetarian, one of my joys, the main one, is that I get to eat a *lot* of vegetables. I don't eat a lot of pseudo meats and dairy products— why would I when there are beans, nuts, grains, and the green and glorious Vegetable Kingdom!?* What vegetarian me does eat for dinner is a slice of good rustic toast or a bowl of rice or noodles with two or three tasty vegetable concoctions, like the ones in this chapter. Smart vegetarian me knows the value of leftovers and so makes enough to last for a couple of days of eating in a couple of ways.

* See Bryant Terry's *Vegetable Kingdom* for *all* the glories!

BROCCO TACOS

I'll admit it: Broccoli is my cabbage. By which I mean: You know how cabbage is so much a staple vegetable the world round, the one that's reached for—roasted, boiled, pickled, fermented, stuffed, wrapped, raw—reached for so much that it's almost not an ingredient, it just is? Broccoli is like that for me. Of course, cabbage's immense popularity is due in no small part to its longevity. Broccoli won't keep as long, but it does pretty well in the fridge and, as long as it's not yellowing or smelling strong, can be brought back to life if handled right. For me that's always, or mostly, browned in a skillet with a good amount of oil and salt. Sometimes with a lid, sometimes with a splash of water. When it's quite cooked, which is the way I like it, the parade of versions can begin. With lots of garlic and pasta or rice, naturally, or alongside meat if that what's going on. On a tortilla kick recently I stumbled, hungry, past lunchtime, into Brocco Tacos and, like that, a new broccoli branch opened up. Broccoli is the meat of the taco, made meatier if you like with actual meats like bacon, sausage, or anchovies, or with eggs, tofu, pumpkin seeds, sesame seeds, or nuts. Beans ought to be involved, either crushed in with the broccoli or refried separately. Grated cheese, fresh cilantro, chopped lettuce, tomatoes, scallions, salsa . . . you know, tacos.

MAKES ENOUGH FOR 6ISH TACOS

¼ cup cooking oil, olive or vegetable, plus more as needed (see Tips, page 7)

1 head of broccoli, florets cut from stems, big stems peeled, little ones discarded, everything cut into pieces of the same size

Fine sea salt or kosher salt

2 garlic cloves, finely chopped

Crushed red pepper flakes

1 teaspoon whole cumin seeds (optional; see Tips, page 8)

Corn tortillas

Heat a large skillet (see Tips, page 6) over high heat, add the oil, then add the broccoli right away. Sprinkle with salt and stir. Reduce the heat to medium, cover, and cook, stirring occasionally, adding a bit of oil if it seems dry or a splash of water if it's getting too browned before fully cooked. When tasting for doneness, think about salt too.

Move the broccoli to one side when done and add the garlic, red pepper flakes, and cumin (if using) to the other side, with a little more oil if it needs it. Cook till it smells great but the garlic doesn't get browned at all, about 20 seconds, then stir everything together.

Serve with warmed tortillas (I just toast them, turning with tongs over an open gas flame—a toaster oven or dry skillet works well too), the stuff mentioned above, and the other stuff you like to put in tacos.

(continued)

Variations

- If adding bacon or sausage, cut or crumble and cook that first, set aside, and use the same skillet to proceed with the broccoli, adding the meat back in at the end.
- Eggs can be whisked up, with salt and a little milk if you like, and gently scrambled in with the finished broccoli. Alternatively, silken tofu can be stirred in at this point.
- Toasted seeds and nuts can be stirred into the finished broccoli.
- Turn the warm broccoli out into a bowl and stir in ricotta or crumbled feta or queso fresco.
- Combinations! All of the above would be . . . a lot, but probably pretty great.

REGULAR ONIONS WITH HOISIN AND SHAOXING WINE

The ubiquitous onion has long been my mascot ingredient. Here I hope to take some sweet steps toward bringing it to full vegetable status. I generally use yellow onions here, but white or red would be fine. Throw in some cubed tofu at the end and this is dinner. Regular Onions also make a nice accompaniment to meats, especially pork.

MAKES 2 ONIONS' WORTH—AND IS A VERY USEFUL LEFTOVER

2 medium yellow onions

¼ cup cooking oil, olive or vegetable (see Tips, page 7), or butter

Fine sea salt or kosher salt

¼ cup Shaoxing wine or dry sherry

2 tablespoons hoisin sauce, or more if you like it a little . . . more

Handful of fresh cilantro sprigs, leaves and stems, chopped (optional)

Trim the ends off the onions and cut them in half pole to pole. Peel them and trim away any irregular parts. Cut the onions into thick wedges.

Heat a large skillet (see Tips, page 6) over high heat and add the oil and onions right away. Sprinkle with salt and stir. Cook for a few minutes, until browning begins to happen, then stir and brown some more. Continue for 5 minutes, then add the wine—be careful; sometimes the wine can ignite, which is fine, and dramatic, but step back a bit. Let the wine bubble for 30 seconds or so, then add the hoisin and 1 cup water. Reduce the heat to a simmer and cook until tender, about 10 minutes, adding more water as needed to keep the onions moist and stewy. Sprinkle in the cilantro, if using.

ONION RINGINGS

I guess it's a good thing that deep-frying is sort of a pain to do at home and away from the Fryolator. Fried things are so irresistible that if it weren't for the mess, we'd be frying a lot more, and that might be too much. Still, it is worth it to deal with the hassle once in a while, especially if it means onion rings. Here are three versions, none hard, all messy. See Tips (page 11) for suggestions for how to dispose of used oil.

SKAKET BEACH THINS

I never knew beach onion rings were a thing until I went to Skaket Beach on Cape Cod. I didn't wonder why, just got plenty of ketchup, competed enthusiastically with the gulls and boys, and then dove in the bay to wash away the slick of grease and a tiny spot of guilt.

MAKES 2 TO 4 SERVINGS

1 medium yellow onion

Fine sea salt or kosher salt

Beer

Oil for frying—rice bran, grape seed, or other vegetable oil (see Tips, page 7)

1 cup all-purpose flour

Ketchup (optional—or is it?)

Put a baking sheet in the oven and heat the oven to 200°F for keeping the onion rings warm as you fry in batches (or just eat them as you go). Make sure you have ready a spider or slotted spoon for lifting the rings from the oil when done, and a wire rack or a tray lined with crumpled paper for them to land on.

Slice the onion as thinly as you can into rings. Mix the rings with ½ teaspoon salt and the beer and set aside for 5 minutes.

In a medium pot, bring 3 inches of oil to 375°F over medium heat.

Put the flour in a large bowl. Using one hand, lift about a quarter of the onion rings from the beer and let the excess drip off. Drop them into the flour and use the other hand to toss them until well coated. This two-handed technique keeps your fingers on one hand from getting battered. Well, mostly.

Check the oil to see if it's at frying temperature, 375°F. If you don't have a thermometer, drop a ring in to test fry. If it sinks and bubbles just a little or not at all, it's not hot enough. If it makes you jump back, it's too hot and you'll have to wait till it calms down before proceeding.

Use your hand again to lift the rings from the flour, shake off the excess, and carefully add to the hot oil. Fry until golden brown, 2 to 3 minutes. Transfer to the rack or paper to drain, sprinkle with salt, eat some, and keep the rest warm in the oven while you fry the remaining batches.

Eat hot. If you need a sauce that isn't ketchup, try the Red Bean MUFU sauce (page 50).

YOGURT RINGS

Buttermilk works for these as well, but I find that I have yogurt in the fridge more often. Either way, they have a little richness and a nice tang.

MAKES 2 TO 4 SERVINGS

1 medium yellow onion

Fine sea salt or kosher salt

Oil for frying—rice bran, grape seed, or other vegetable oil (see Tips, page 7)

¼ cup plain whole-milk yogurt

1 cup all-purpose flour, plus more as needed

Ketchup (optional—or is it?)

One of the yogurt sauces (page 134)

Put a baking sheet in the oven and heat the oven to 200°F for keeping the onion rings warm as you fry in batches (or just eat them as you go). Make sure you have ready a spider or slotted spoon for lifting the rings from the oil when done, and a wire rack or a tray lined with crumpled paper for them to land on.

Slice the onion into ½- to ¾-inch rings. In a large bowl, sprinkle the onion slices with ½ teaspoon salt. Set aside for 5 minutes.

In a medium pot, bring 3 inches of oil to 375°F over medium heat.

Add the yogurt to the onions and turn to coat well. Put the flour in a large bowl. Using one hand, lift about a quarter of the onion rings from the yogurt and let the excess drip off. Drop them into the flour and use the other hand to toss them until well coated. This two-handed technique keeps your fingers on one hand from getting battered. Well, mostly.

Check the oil to see if it's at frying temperature, 375°F. If you don't have a thermometer, drop a ring in to test fry. If it sinks and bubbles just a little or not at all, it's not hot enough. If it makes you jump back, it's too hot and you'll have to wait till it calms down before proceeding.

Use your hand again to lift the rings from the flour, shake off the excess, and carefully add to the hot oil. Fry until golden brown, 2 to 3 minutes. Transfer to the rack or paper to drain, sprinkle with salt, eat some, and keep the rest warm in the oven while you fry the remaining batches. Add more flour if needed for coating them.

Eat hot with ketchup or yogurt sauce.

GLUTEN-FREE NOT-RINGS

Cut into wedges, just for fun. Rings would work too, of course.

MAKES 2 TO 4 SERVINGS

1 medium yellow onion

Fine sea salt or kosher salt

Oil for frying—rice bran, grape seed, or other vegetable oil (see Tips, page 7)

½ cup chickpea flour, plus more as needed

½ cup rice flour, plus more as needed

¼ teaspoon baking soda

2 teaspoons ground turmeric

1 teaspoon sweet paprika

Bubbly water (or tap water if bubbly is not available)

Ketchup (optional—or is it?)

One of the vegetable puree sauces (page 126; optional)

Put a baking sheet in the oven and heat the oven to 200°F for keeping the onion wedges warm as you fry in batches (or just eat them as you go). Make sure you have ready a spider or slotted spoon for lifting the wedges from the oil when done, and a wire rack or a tray lined with crumpled paper for them to land on.

Cut the onion into ¾-inch-thick wedges, leaving a little bit of the root end on so the layers stay attached. (Don't worry if they come apart—also fine.) Sprinkle the onion wedges with ½ teaspoon salt and set aside for 5 minutes.

In a medium pot, bring 3 inches of oil to 375°F over medium heat.

Meanwhile, make the batter: In a large bowl, combine the flours, baking soda, turmeric, paprika, and a pinch of salt. Whisk in enough bubbly water to make a batter the consistency of yogurt. Dip an onion wedge to see if the batter is right—if it's too thick and clumpy, add water; if it's too thin and runs right off, add more of the flours.

Check the oil to see if it's at frying temperature, 375°F. If you don't have a thermometer, drop a piece of onion in to test fry. If it sinks and bubbles just a little or not at all, it's not hot enough. If it makes you jump back, it's too hot and you'll have to wait till it calms down before proceeding.

Use your fingers to lift the onions from the batter, allow the excess to drip off, and carefully add to the hot oil. Fry until golden brown, 2 to 3 minutes. Transfer to the rack or paper to drain, sprinkle with salt, eat some, and keep the rest warm in the oven while you fry the remaining batches.

Eat hot with ketchup or vegetable puree sauce.

CELERY SWOOSHES WITH PEANUTS AND GINGER

I do love a salad made with humble celery. This dressing is also good with cucumbers, tomatoes, thinly sliced raw peppers, and briefly boiled cauliflower or broccoli.

MAKES 4 SERVINGS

Fine sea salt or kosher salt

2 tablespoons finely chopped shallot or red onion or the white part of a scallion

½ inch of fresh ginger, grated or finely chopped (about 1 teaspoon)

Finely chopped jalapeño or other hot chile to taste

Grated zest of half a lime

Juice of 1 lime

1 teaspoon rice vinegar

2 teaspoons peanut butter, chunky or smooth

Cayenne or other finely ground hot pepper to taste

3 tablespoons vegetable oil or mild olive oil

6 celery stalks, leaves and root ends removed, thinly sliced on an angle for the swoosh

¼ cup chopped fresh cilantro leaves and stems (optional)

¼ cup roasted peanuts, roughly chopped (optional)

Bring a medium saucepan of salted water to a boil over high heat. **Meanwhile,** make the dressing: in a small bowl, stir together the shallot, ginger, jalapeño, lime zest and juice, vinegar, peanut butter, cayenne, and ⅛ teaspoon salt. Stir in the oil and set aside.

Add the celery swooshes to the boiling water and cook until just tender but with lots of crunch, about 3 minutes. Drain and cool.

Combine the cooled celery with most of the dressing. Mix in the cilantro and peanuts, if using. Taste and adjust with salt and maybe more dressing. Eat right away, or it will also hold, refrigerated or not, for a few hours.

MUSHROOMS WITH HONEY AND CORIANDER

Older mushrooms, ones that have opened to reveal dark gills, tend to cook up a little murky. I've tried freshening them with cream, which seemed to make them look worse, like when floodwaters turn not just the bottom but the entire river to mud. In an easy spirit of trying less pushing back and more going with, I brought in honey, for its sweet funk when cooked, and coriander, to root the floral in the earth. Grind on black pepper for kick, and if you have mint, fresh or even dried, like for tea, it's very good with mushrooms.

Eat hot with rice, with scrambled eggs or in an omelet, or spooned over chicken. Gets arguably better after refrigerating for a day or two.

MAKES 5 SERVINGS

2 tablespoons honey

1 scant tablespoon coriander seeds, crushed, or 1 scant teaspoon ground coriander (see Tips, page 8)

2 tablespoons sliced fresh mint leaves or 1 teaspoon dried mint leaves

3 tablespoons cooking oil, olive or vegetable (see Tips, page 7)

1 pound button mushrooms (or oyster, king trumpet, shiitake, or wild mushrooms), trimmed, quartered, and rinsed

1 generous teaspoon fine sea salt or kosher salt

Juice of 1 lemon

Ground black pepper

Put the honey in a skillet that's large enough to fit the mushrooms. Heat over medium heat until the honey melts, then add the coriander and mint. Stir for 30 seconds, then add the oil, mushrooms, and salt. Cook, stirring occasionally, until the mushrooms are tender, 10 to 15 minutes. Add a splash of water if things are getting sizzly and overcaramelized. Stir in the lemon juice and black pepper, taste, and adjust.

CELERY BAKED WITH BLACK PEPPER, BACON, AND CREAM

Go ahead, say it: Sure, cook anything with bacon and cream and it will taste good.

Go ahead, say it: I do not like celery.

Now admit it: Celery tastes good.

MAKES 4 TO 6 SERVINGS

1 head of celery

Fine sea salt or kosher salt

3 bacon slices, cut across into ½-inch-wide strips

½ cup light or heavy cream (but not half-and-half; it will break)

1 cup grated Parmesan or Grana Padano cheese

2 tablespoons chopped fresh parsley leaves

Ground black pepper

Fresh or toasted bread (optional)

Heat the oven to 450°F.

Bring a large pot of water to a boil over high heat. The pot should be big enough for the celery to fit in with plenty of room to swim. Add salt.

Meanwhile, trim away and discard any brown parts or floppy outer stalks from the head of celery and cut off just enough of the root end so that the stalks separate. Wash to get rid of any grit, then cut the stalks on a diagonal into 1-inch lengths—I like to use the inner stalks and any leaves as well.

Boil the celery until tender with very little bite, 4 to 6 minutes. Drain and set aside.

Heat a large skillet (see Tips, page 6) over medium heat, add the bacon, and cook until rendered and browning, 3 to 4 minutes. Spoon off some of the fat if you need to—I usually don't—and add the cream. Turn off the heat and stir to get any stuck bits of bacon.

In a large bowl, combine the celery, cream-bacon mixture, grated cheese, and parsley and grind in lots of black pepper. Stir well and pour into a baking dish or oven-going skillet— maybe the one you cooked the bacon in—and bake until golden on top and the cream has thickened, 20 to 30 minutes. Serve solo with fresh bread or toast or as a side dish.

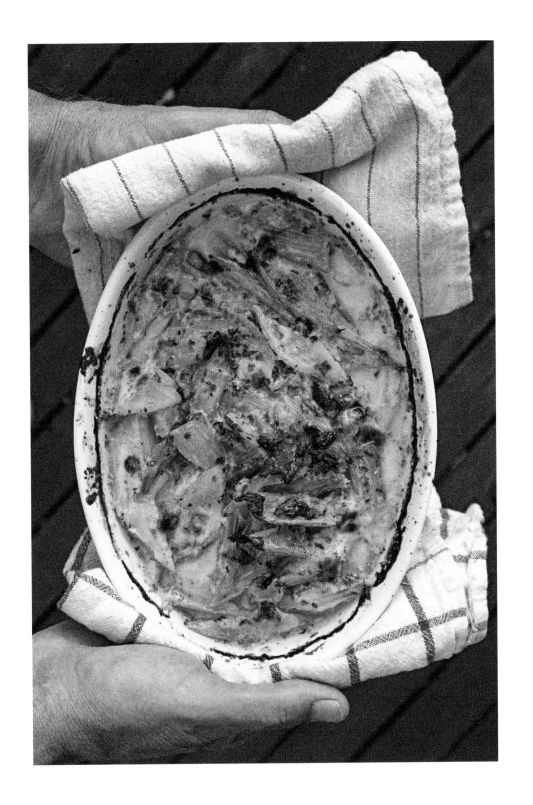

ROASTED RADISHES WITH CHILES, LIME, AND FISH SAUCE

When radishes get too big, bland, or boring, give them this treatment. Or even when they are in great shape, crunch on some raw while the others roast. Watermelon radishes, more and more findable at farmers' markets and Asian groceries, are delicious and look very cool-pink done this way.

Eat at room temperature or chilled as a salad or hot from the oven with rice, beans, chickpeas, chicken, or pork.

MAKES 4 SERVINGS

8 Ping-Pong ball–size radishes (organic, if possible), quartered*

4 tablespoons cooking oil, olive or vegetable (see Tips, page 7)

Jalapeño or other fresh hot chile, sliced and seeded (or not), or crushed red pepper flakes, to taste

¼ teaspoon fine sea salt or kosher salt

2 teaspoons fish sauce

Juice of 1 lime

¼ cup roasted peanuts, chopped or crushed

2 tablespoons roughly chopped fresh cilantro leaves and tender stems

Heat the oven to 450°F. Line a baking sheet with parchment paper.

In a large bowl, toss the radishes with 2 tablespoons of the oil, the chiles, and the salt. Spread the radishes on the baking sheet and roast until tender and lightly browned, 10 to 15 minutes. Return the roasted radishes to the bowl and toss with the remaining 2 tablespoons oil, the fish sauce, lime juice, peanuts, and cilantro. Taste and adjust.

....

* Or use a mix of radish types, cutting the bigger ones down to the littler ones' size so they roast at the same rate.

GLAZED CARROT PHALANGES
(A.K.A. BABY CARROTS)

Baby carrots are not literally baby carrots. They are a special slender, tender variety of regular grown-up carrots, sawed into pieces and rolled creepily smooth in a tumbler. Also, baby carrots present a choking hazard and are *not* safe for babies. So I call them phalanges—finger segments. I added almonds because I love them with carrots and—Halloween bonus—they look like fingernails! Crushed red pepper included for spice and gore.

MAKES 4 SERVINGS

3 tablespoons unsalted butter

2 tablespoons lightly packed light or dark brown sugar

1 inch of fresh ginger, chopped (about 1 tablespoon)

1 pound carrot phalanges (organic, if possible)

½ teaspoon fine sea salt or kosher salt

2 teaspoons red wine vinegar (or other vinegar)

Ground black pepper

Crushed red pepper flakes

½ cup sliced almonds, toasted (see Tips, page 8)

In a large coverable skillet (see Tips, page 6), melt the butter and brown sugar over medium heat. When they get all bubbly, add the ginger and sizzle for 10 seconds. Add the phalanges, salt, and ¾ cup water and bring to a boil. Reduce the heat to a lively simmer and cook, covered, until tender, about 12 minutes. Add more water if needed. Uncover and continue cooking until the liquid is reduced to a syrup. Stir in the vinegar, black pepper, red pepper flakes, and almonds. Taste, adjust, and serve.

CARROTS ROASTED IN THE AFTERMATH

I always did my best to take a gourmet hiatus when laying out the spread for our kids' birthday parties, indulging their (and, secretly, my) yearning for cheesy crunchies, ranchy munchies, and neon sweeties. When nutritional guilt would swell and threaten to burst like a piñata full of Snickers, I'd grab a peeler and start making a raw vegetable platter—even the candied palates of ten-year-olds must require some roughage, I'd reason. After, when the only thing left standing in the debris field of torn wrappers and crushed doodles was my crudité, perfectly intact, I deflected the adolescent I-told-you-so looks and lit the oven.

"You'll eat these vegetables," I'd mutter, sweeping the entire platter into a mixing bowl and getting louder, "Roasted, with chermoula, the North African herb sauce!"

"What," my wife would ask, arms full of empty snack bowls, kids in retreat, "are you yelling about?"

"Chermoula," I'd say, volume lowered by mouthfuls of crow and M&M's, knowing she'd heard it before, "the North African herb sauce."

MAKES 4 TO 6 SERVINGS AND EXTRA CHERMOULA

1 bunch of fresh cilantro, stems and leaves roughly chopped

1 garlic clove, finely grated or chopped with salt to paste (see Tips, page 7)

1 inch of fresh ginger, finely grated or chopped (about 1 tablespoon)

¾ cup olive oil

Fine sea salt or kosher salt

1 pound carrots, peeled and cut as if kids were going to healthfully devour them, or a party platter of carrots, celery, radishes, broccoli, and so on

1 lime

Heat the oven to 450°F.

To make the chermoula, combine the cilantro, garlic, ginger, oil, and ¼ teaspoon salt in a blender jar and whiz until just smooth. It's better to undermix than overmix—it's okay if it's a little chunky.

In a large bowl, sprinkle the carrots with ¼ teaspoon salt and half the chermoula sauce and stir to coat well. Spread the carrots on a baking sheet and roast until tender, about 15 minutes. Squeeze lime juice on the carrots and call the kids.

Nice as a side dish or with rice or couscous and a spoonful of plain yogurt. Leftover chermoula will keep for a few days in the fridge and is good on everything.

MESS OF SCALLIONS

If you can ever get your hands on a mess of chives, this works great with them too, maybe better (see Variations below). Eat with rice or as a side/salsa with meats, chicken, or soft cheese.

MAKES 4 SERVINGS

¼ cup cooking oil, olive or vegetable (see Tips, page 7), plus more as needed

3 bunches of scallions, green *and* white parts, sliced into 1½-inch pieces

½ teaspoon fine sea salt or kosher salt

2 teaspoons red wine vinegar or sherry vinegar

2 tablespoons currants or raisins, soaked in hot water until plumped

2 tablespoons unsalted butter

Heat a large skillet (see Tips, page 6) over medium-high heat. Add the oil, then the scallions right away. Add the salt, reduce the heat to medium, and cook, stirring occasionally, until well-browned and approaching burnt, about 10 minutes. Add a splash of water if needed to get them tender or a jot of oil if the skillet seems to be getting dry. Turn off the heat and allow to cool somewhat, then stir in the vinegar, currants, and butter.

Variations

- If using chives, cut them into 2- to 3-inch lengths and cook a little less—taste for tenderness.
- Instead of currants or raisins, try adding 1 heaping tablespoon toasted sesame seeds, a couple teaspoons of soy sauce, a tablespoon of oyster sauce, and a splash of rice wine vinegar or other vinegar. Add some cubes of tofu and this is a meal.

SCALLION DIP

I got my first real kiss playing spin the bottle at a blacklight-lit party in Anne-Marie's basement. A stick of strawberry incense trailed smoke in the corner. We were in wide-wale flairs, Bay City Rollin' down the Yellow Brick Road to high school, and though I remember well the snacks— Doritos, Peanut M&M's, and Ruffles with French onion dip—I can't quite remember the sequence of events that night. I just hope the French kiss happened *before* the French dip. If not, a long-overdue apology to Anne-Marie.

MAKES 2 CUPS

¼ cup cooking oil, olive or vegetable (see Tips, page 7)

1 medium yellow onion, diced

Fine sea salt or kosher salt

1 bunch of scallions, green *and* white parts, sliced into ½-inch pieces

1 teaspoon Worcestershire sauce

1 teaspoon soy sauce

1 cup sour cream

Heat a large skillet (see Tips, page 6) over high heat and add the oil, then the onion and ½ teaspoon salt. Stir until it gets going, then reduce the heat to medium and cook, stirring occasionally, until the onion is softened, but not entirely, 8 to 10 minutes. Add the scallions and ¼ teaspoon salt, reduce the heat to low, cover, and continue cooking, stirring occasionally, until dark and jammy, about 20 minutes. What some might call burnt bits are more than okay. Put the scallion mixture in a medium bowl, stir in the Worcestershire and soy sauces, and allow to cool completely. Stir in the sour cream, taste, and adjust with salt and Worcestershire. Serve in the basement with Ruffles. Have some M&M's before kissing anyone.

BAKED POTATOES AND SURROGATE FRIES

No recipe needed, I know, but I'm stanning the venerable baked potato for two reasons:

- **One,** it's super-easy to prepare, and a buttered baked potato, combined with two or three of the other recipes in this chapter, makes a nice meal. Also great with a dollop of Scallion Dip (page 102). (My potato baking method, by the way: Heat the oven to 450°F. Rinse russet potatoes and place them directly on the oven rack. No poking, no foil. Bake until soft all the way through, about an hour.)
- **Two,** I love French fries, but not enough to go through all the steps to make them at home, so I always bake a few extra potatoes. The next day, I cut them into wedges and shallow- or deep-fry them up into a very acceptable surrogate fry to dip in Ranch Dressing (page 71) or one of the MUFU sauces (page 45).

MEAT NOT CUTE

Everybody has a butt. No matter
what size it is, you can work it.
—BIG FREEDIA

I know Big Freedia is not talking about Boston butt and other cuts, but her wisdom applies—it's what you've got and you have to work it, no matter the size, no matter the quality. Still, this chapter will be brief, because eating secret meat of mysterious circumstances is an indulgence, if it can be called that, that should be undertaken only rarely. I try to always cook with the very best meats I can find and afford—that is, meat from animals that are raised like I, and you, would raise them—but I am not pretending that that is always possible. Nor am I suggesting that you seek out lesser meats for these recipes, but when you inevitably end up with something too bland, too lean, too tough, or too long sealed in a plastic package (works for storage, not great for quality), here's how to make the most of it.

BS CHICKEN THIGHS

We've all been there, deep in the enjoyment of crisp and juicy poultry skin and there, on the rim of a dinnermate's plate, that same luscious skin lying rejected, intentionally picked off! Inexplicable, but if chicken skin must be omitted, I suppose the thigh is the part that can weather it best. Here are some of the ways to make the deficit all right.

DIJON CHICKEN THIGHS ROYALE

Mustard was once declared my crutch by a surly, competitive kitchen comrade. I own it and am proud to lean on it once again here. Think of this Dijon sauce not as a cover but rather a cloak, a golden one that does the very best it can to make whatever lies beneath it end up looking a queen.

MAKES 6 SERVINGS

1½ pounds boneless, skinless chicken thighs, whole or cut into big chunks (see Tips, page 10)

1 teaspoon fine sea salt or kosher salt

Ground black pepper

2 tablespoons Dijon mustard

3 tablespoons all-purpose flour, plus more as needed

2 tablespoons unsalted butter

¼ cup cooking oil, olive or vegetable (see Tips, page 7)

1 heaping tablespoon mustard seeds—black, brown, and/or yellow

1 large yellow onion, diced

2 or 3 celery stalks, thinly sliced

1 bay leaf

¾ cup dry white wine or beer

Cooked rice or buttered noodles, for serving

Sour cream or crème fraîche (optional)

Chopped fresh herbs such as parsley, dill, and/or thyme (optional)

In a large bowl, sprinkle the chicken all over with a generous teaspoon of salt. Grind on plenty of black pepper, add the mustard, and turn to coat well. Set aside at room temperature for up to an hour to let the seasonings take hold, or refrigerate for longer, up to overnight. If refrigerating, it's good to let the chicken, and all meats, come to room temperature before cooking.

Heat the oven to 450°F.

Add the flour to the bowl and stir until the chicken pieces are well coated, being sure to unfold any folds so flour can get in there. Add a spoonful more flour if needed to cover any bare spots.

Heat a large skillet (see Tips, page 6) over medium-high heat and add the butter and 2 tablespoons of the oil. When the butter has melted, begin adding the floured chicken pieces to the skillet, shaking them first to leave excess flour behind. Brown one side well, then the other, about 8 minutes per side. Set aside on a plate while you repeat with the

(continued)

remaining pieces of chicken, then remove them to the plate as well. Don't worry about the chicken getting cooked through at this point—it will finish in the oven. Nice golden browning is the important thing.

If the skillet has gotten very dark, wipe it or rinse it before proceeding. Over medium heat, add the remaining 2 tablespoons oil and the mustard seeds. Let the seeds sizzle in the time it takes to turn and grab the onion and celery and add them to the skillet. Sprinkle with ¼ teaspoon salt, add the bay leaf, and cook, stirring occasionally, until the onion is softened and turning un-opaque, about 10 minutes. Add the wine and 1½ cups water and bring to a boil. Fit the chicken into the skillet if it is oven-going, otherwise pour the mixture into a casserole and snuggle the chicken into the liquid.

Bake for 10 minutes, then reduce the heat to 325°F. Cook until very tender and the liquid has thickened, about 30 minutes more. Add a splash of water if the sauce is too thick. Taste, adjust, and serve hot with rice or spooned over buttered noodles. Nice with a sprinkle of herbs and a dollop of sour cream or crème fraîche stirred in.

CHIPOTLE CHICKEN THIGHS WITH CUMIN AND HONEY

I have never understood barbecue sauce. Why coat your chicken with a substance that seems engineered to make it burn on the grill? It's too sweet and too goopy, and inevitably, it's burnt. But I'm not against the coming together of sweet, savory, and spicy, like in this recipe that bakes up easily in the oven with cumin and coriander seeds that are crushed but not powdered—I like the little textural pop they give this way.

Unless you are scaling this recipe up to feed sixty instead of six, there is actually no way that you want to use the whole can of chipotles (feel free to take that as a challenge, you thrill seekers). Taste a piece of one of the peppers to gauge its fire—they vary considerably, like all chiles—and then use the amount that seems right to you. Luckily, chipotles in adobo keep well in the fridge for a week or so (or longer in the freezer) and provide incentive to make it again and perfect your moves.

MAKES 6 SERVINGS

1½ pounds boneless, skinless chicken thighs (see Tips, page 10)

1 teaspoon fine sea salt or kosher salt

1 tablespoon toasted and crushed cumin seeds (see Tips, page 8)

1 tablespoon toasted and crushed coriander seeds (see Tips, page 8)

2 tablespoons honey

Part of a 7-ounce can of chipotle peppers in adobo sauce, finely chopped, pounded, or pureed (a quarter of a can will achieve popular spiciness)

2 tablespoons cooking oil, olive or vegetable (see Tips, page 7)

Cilantro, for strewing

Limes, for squeezing

Brussels sprouts puree (page 128; optional)

Heat the oven to 450°F.

If the thighs are all the same size, cool. Otherwise cut the big ones into pieces to match the small. On a sheet pan or in a baking dish big enough to hold the chicken in a single layer, sprinkle the chicken all over with the salt, cumin, and coriander.

In a large bowl, stir together the honey, chipotles, and oil. Add the chicken to the bowl and coat well.

Spread the chicken on the sheet pan and bake until browned and cooked through, 15 to 20 minutes. Cut into a thigh and take a peek to see that it's done.

Roughly chop plenty of cilantro, stems and all, and strew over the chicken. Serve with wedges of lime and/or with Brussels sprouts puree (page 128).

CREAMY CHICKEN RAGÙ: CHEESE GRATER EDITION

The only time anyone has ever used the spiky little stars side of my box grater was when one of the kids was pretending Play-Doh was Parmesan. That was many years ago, and the nuggets of blue and orange are still there, petrified reminders to never use that side—you grate and grate and the chunk of cheese in your hand gets smaller, yet your spaghetti goes unsprinkled while the cheese seems to mysteriously disappear. You can imagine it passing into a parallel universe where golden Parmesan drifts down like snow, or you can just use the other side of the grater.

For this recipe I eschew knife and cutting board for dicing onion, carrots, and celery into tiny cubes—my usual, and usually enjoyable technique—and instead do the whole process using the big-hole side of my box grater, directly into the skillet that I'll be cooking in.

MAKES 4 SERVINGS

1½ pounds boneless, skinless chicken thighs (see Tips, page 10)

1½ teaspoons fine sea salt or kosher salt

Ground black pepper

1 medium yellow onion

1 large carrot, peeled

2 celery stalks

One 15-ounce can whole peeled tomatoes, with their juices

2 garlic cloves, peeled and halved

¼ cup cooking oil, olive or vegetable (see Tips, page 7)

¾ cup light or heavy cream (but not half-and-half; it will break)

Pasta, rice, or toast, for serving

Heat the oven to 350°F.

Sprinkle the chicken thighs with 1 teaspoon of the salt and lots of black pepper. Set aside at room temperature.

Set a box grater in an oven-safe skillet large enough to hold the chicken thighs and use the big-hole side to grate the onion, carrot, celery, and tomatoes into the skillet. Add the garlic, the remaining ½ teaspoon salt, the oil, cream, and 1½ cups water. Add the chicken thighs and bring to a bubbling simmer over high heat, stirring once or twice, then place the skillet in the oven and bake until the chicken is very tender and the liquid has thickened, 30 to 40 minutes.

Remove the skillet from the oven. You can just stir vigorously to shred the chicken, or remove it, chop it, and return to the sauce. Taste and adjust, adding more water if too thick.

Serve stirred with al dente pasta or spooned over rice or thick slices of toast.

BS CHICKEN BREAST, EASY-FRIED TWO WAYS

Boneless, skinless . . . might as well throw in fun-less while they're at it. Curiously, chicken breasts are often sold this way, and I try not to wonder why too much—why take away those good parts? I never wonder what they do with all that skin and bone.

However. Here you are with your package, and your hope, and you will not be let down. First you just need to deal with your feelings around the fact that there will be no crispy brown skin. Accept it and hear the ways you can mitigate this disappointment.

BS CHICKEN BREAST, DORATO-STYLE

Reversing the usual egg then flour, this method makes for fried chicken that is sunny-side golden, or *dorato*.

MAKES 4 SERVINGS

1½ pounds boneless, skinless chicken breasts (see Tips, page 10)

1 teaspoon fine sea salt or kosher salt

Ground black pepper

1 egg

All-purpose flour

Cooking oil, olive or vegetable (see Tips, page 7)

Optional for serving: lemon wedges; or tomato sauce and grated Parmesan or Grana Padano cheese; or hazelnut salsa (page 130); or green bean puree (page 128)

Put a baking sheet in the oven and heat the oven to 200°F to keep the chicken warm as you fry in batches.

Season the chicken with the salt and grind on some black pepper. If the breasts are more than an inch thick, smack them with your hand or a clean heavy object (skillet, mallet, cutting board) to pound thinner. In one shallow bowl, whisk the egg. In another, put a scoop of flour—enough to coat the chicken. Place half the chicken breasts in the flour and turn to coat completely. Shake off the excess and then turn the pieces in the egg to coat completely. Heat a large skillet (see Tips, page 6) to medium-high and add ¼ inch of oil.

Lift the chicken breasts from the egg, let drip, and then carefully place into the hot oil. Fry until golden, about 5 minutes, then flip and do the other side for another 5 minutes, or until nicely browned and cooked through—use a knife to cut a slit into the thickest part and sneak a peek to be sure. Keep warm in the oven as you fry the rest.

Delicious with just a squeeze of lemon or with a simple tomato sauce blanket and shower of grated Parmesan or Grana Padano cheese. Or with hazelnut salsa or green bean puree.

BS CHICKEN BREAST, TANGY AND TURMERICAL

For chicken that is also decidedly golden, this deep-fry method works with traditional buttermilk or, my preference, trusty yogurt. Turmerical chicken with hot chickpeas (Garbonanza MUFU, page 48) or lentils, some chopped scallions and cilantro, a squeeze of lime, and some hot sauce is a simple dinner with wow. Some like it with mash, others cole slaw—I like to eat turmerical chicken next-day-cold, standing in the kitchen, with pickles and beer. Always good and extra yellow with cauliflower puree (page 126) too.

MAKES 4 SERVINGS

Oil for frying—rice bran, grape seed, or other vegetable oil (see Tips, page 7)

1½ pounds boneless, skinless chicken breasts (see Tips, page 10)

1 teaspoon fine sea salt or kosher salt

Ground black pepper

6 tablespoons plain whole-milk yogurt or buttermilk

2 teaspoons ground turmeric

2 teaspoons toasted sesame seeds (see Tips, page 8)

1 teaspoon sweet or hot paprika

½ cup all-purpose flour, plus more as needed

Put a baking sheet in the oven and heat the oven to 200°F to keep the chicken warm as you fry in batches.

In a medium pot, bring 3 inches of oil to 375°F over medium heat. Alternately, you can fry with less oil in a skillet (see Tips, page 6).

In a medium bowl, season the chicken breasts with the salt and grind on some black pepper. Add the yogurt, turmeric, sesame seeds, and paprika and coat well. Add the flour and use your hands to thoroughly coat the chicken. Use a spoonful more flour if needed to cover any wet spots.

Working in batches, lift the chicken and shake off any excess flour, then carefully add to the hot oil. Cook until golden brown and cooked through—8 to 10 minutes, but use a knife to cut a slit into the thickest part and sneak a peek to be sure. Keep warm in the oven as you fry the rest.

Variation

Skip the turmeric, paprika, and sesame seeds but use plenty of black pepper. Serve with pecan salsa (page 130).

SPICE-ENCRUSTED BS CHICKEN BREAST ROAST

Larger chicken breasts work best for this one. Be sure to let them rest in a warm spot for 5 or 10 minutes before slicing thin. Good eaten hot with the starch and vegetable/salad you love best and spoonings of cashew salsa (page 134), almond salsa (page 130), or carrot puree (page 126). Also makes a great sandwich folded into a pita with any of the yogurt sauces (page 134) and cucumbers, scallions, tomatoes, cilantro, mint, basil . . .

MAKES 4 SERVINGS

1½ pounds boneless, skinless chicken breasts (see Tips, page 10)

1½ teaspoons fine sea salt or kosher salt

Ground black pepper

2 teaspoons ground turmeric

2 teaspoons ground or whole cumin seeds (see Tips, page 8)

2 teaspoons crushed or ground coriander seeds (see Tips, page 8)

1 teaspoon crushed or ground fennel seeds (see Tips, page 8)

2 tablespoons cooking oil, olive or vegetable (see Tips, page 7)

A while before you plan for the chicken to hit the skillet, preferably ½ hour to 2 hours, season the chicken breasts with the salt, grindings of black pepper, and the turmeric, cumin, coriander, and fennel.

Heat the oven to 450°F.

Heat a large oven-safe skillet (see Tips, page 6) to high, add the oil, and quickly but carefully add the chicken. Reduce the heat to medium-high and cook the chicken until browned, about 5 minutes. Flip over and put the skillet in the oven to roast until the chicken is cooked through. The cooking time will depend on the size of the breasts; use a knife to cut a slit into the thickest part and sneak a peek to be sure. Let rest before slicing and serving.

GRAVY, MEATLOAF, AND MEATBALLS

In her complicated and sorrowful Neapolitan Novels, Elena Ferrante sentences stoic, persuasive, and inscrutable brilliant-friend Lila Cerullo to work in a sausage factory where the conditions are grim and cold and Lila is treated horribly. She suffers and prevails among the dangling salame and mortadelle, and while factory work, especially of the grinding, stuffing, coiling sort, probably deserves to be the allegory for misery that Ferrante makes it, I rather like sausage in particular and ground meats in general.

Ground meats are versatile and take well to assertive seasoning. They are also economically extendable, and might there be a taste of virtue in the careful, respectful use of something so precious and resource-intensive as livestock?

I offer here three recipes that can help with meat that's fine but not *so fine*. When that's what you've ended up with, make one of these: gravy, meatloaf, or meatballs. Though elsewhere I have called meat and tomato–based sauce for pasta *ragù*, here I am calling it *gravy*. I am, after all, from Jersey, but never really got to call the stuff we ate on spaghetti *gravy*—we were more WASPy New Jersey than mobster Joyzee—so I am doing it now, for thrills. Meatloaf and meatballs, like hen and chicks, have significant differences while being essentially made of the same stuff. One cuter and a bit of bother, the other broody, broad, and warm. The recipes are the same for them both, the only difference being shape: loaf or ball. Accompaniments are interchangeable among the three—think of how mashed potatoes, a natural with meatloaf, would work equally well surrounded by merry meatballs or cloaked in meaty gravy.

GRAVY

Pork makes gravy tastier and more succulent, so I use half beef and half pork in this recipe, but you could use all of one or the other if you prefer. I do like the greasy nostalgia that the aroma of sizzling ground beef in a skillet can evoke. It's grassier and less sweet smelling than pork and takes me back to electric skillets and grubby grills whose bad reputations are softened by time and affection. Who can stay mad at the uneven output of a cook with love in his heart, even if he does have gunk on his griddle?

And I use the term *greasy* advisedly and with all respect, the word having picked up a bad reputation that is not entirely, or even at all, deserved. There's little need to enthuse about the tastiness and other culinary charms that animal fats bring to the table—so many great cooks have said so much on the topic, and we thank them. I will say that I was nicely surprised when a nutritionist I was seeing asked me why I wasn't cooking with more lard and duck fat. She went on to recommend her favorite breakfast of gluten-free toast spread with duck fat and topped with smoked duck breast slices. The point is that rendered animal fat is all right, and it does not need to be tipped off and tossed—at least not all of it.

The two pounds of meat called for here makes a lot of gravy, so unless the Sopranos are coming over, you will have enough to freeze for another dinner. Or whack the recipe in half.

MAKES 10 TO 12 SERVINGS

1 pound ground pork (organic, if possible; see Tips, page 10)

1 pound ground beef (grass-fed, if possible; see Tips, page 10)

Fine sea salt or kosher salt

Ground black pepper

2 tablespoons cooking oil, olive or vegetable (see Tips, page 7)

1 medium yellow onion, diced

2 garlic cloves, finely chopped

Crushed red pepper flakes

1 teaspoon chopped fresh thyme leaves (optional)

2 teaspoons chopped fresh oregano leaves or 1 teaspoon dried (optional)

½ cup dry white wine (optional)

One 15-ounce can whole peeled tomatoes, chopped, juices reserved

2 cups chicken, pork, or beef stock, plus more as needed (optional)

½ cup light or heavy cream (but not half-and-half; it will break)

2 tablespoons chopped fresh parsley leaves (optional)

Vinegar—red wine preferred, but white wine works (optional)

On a large plate or platter, spread out the ground meats and sprinkle with 1 teaspoon salt and plenty of ground black pepper. Mix with your hands just until the seasonings are well distributed; overhandling ground meat can make it turn tough, so don't.

Heat a large skillet (see Tips, page 6) over medium-high heat. Add the oil and then quickly add the seasoned meats, spreading them to fill the surface of the skillet. Tilt the pan to spread the oil around if needed, but don't move it around too much—just let it fry. The meat will go from pink to gray and, if you stay out of its way for about 10 minutes, to a nice caramel-brown, which is what you want. When the first side is ready, turn the pieces over and brown the other side, about 5 minutes. Set the meat aside on a plate and tip out some of the grease if you like, but leave at least a couple tablespoons for cooking the onion.

Add the onion to the skillet and sprinkle with ¼ teaspoon salt. Stir with a wooden spoon to scrape up the bits of browned meat as the onion begins to get juicy. Reduce the heat to medium and cook the onion, stirring occasionally, until very tender, about 15 minutes. Add the garlic, red pepper flakes, and the thyme and oregano, if using, and stir for 30 seconds, until the garlic sizzles but doesn't brown. When it smells really good, add the wine, if using, and allow to bubble for a few minutes, then add the chopped tomatoes and a sprinkle of salt and cook, stirring occasionally, for 5 minutes.

Return the ground meats to the skillet, breaking up any chunks that are too large. Add the stock (or 2 cups water), and tomato juice and adjust the heat so that the sauce is simmering but not bubbling fast, and cook for 20 minutes. Taste a piece of meat to see if it is tender—if not, add another cup of stock or water and keep cooking.

Add the cream when the meat doneness seems right, bring back to a simmer, and cook for another 10 minutes. Taste for salt, acidity (a drop of vinegar to counter richness?), and texture—adjustable by further simmering to thicken, adding stock or water to thin.

Serve with pasta. Also makes a nice Sloppy Joe (my Mafia name, btw).

HOT-PATOOTIE MEATLOAF

When you're growing up in the seventies in rural New Jersey, it's not easy to access alternative culture. I found it in books and in movies *about* places far away and then I *got* far away, but before I left I saw many midnight screenings of *The Rocky Horror Picture Show*. I fell in with the theater kids at my high school, and *Rocky Horror* on Saturday night was where we discovered, and embodied, a queer, sexy, silly world that none of the turnpike exits led to. It was a trans, sci-fi place where junkies, extraterrestrials, and monsters danced and sang, the last place you'd expect to find homely meatloaf, but there was homely Meat Loaf! Mr. Loaf had to give a lot to fit into such exotic surroundings, and when you make meatloaf you need to give a lot too. This completely condimental version is strictly for the hamborghese among you.

MAKES 8 SERVINGS

2 pounds ground beef (grass-fed, if possible), or any combination of ground beef, pork, and turkey (see Tips, page 10)

1 teaspoon fine sea salt or kosher salt

Ground black pepper

1 tablespoon Dijon mustard

2 tablespoons ketchup

2 tablespoons mayonnaise

½ cup coarsely chopped pickles

1 small red onion, diced

4 bacon slices, cooked and crumbled

½ cup grated Cheddar cheese

2 cups fresh bread crumbs or 1½ cups dried bread crumbs

2 eggs

Heat the oven to 375°F.

In a large bowl, combine all the ingredients and use your hands to squish them all together. They should be well mixed, but remember that overhandling ground meat can make it turn tough, so don't.

Load into a loaf pan and bake for 45 minutes. Use a meat thermometer to see that the loaf has reached 160°F, or test for doneness by inserting the blade of a knife center-loaf, count to five, pull out the knife, and feel the blade on the back of your hand. If it is anything other than hot, keep cooking the meatloaf for another 10 minutes or so. Ask who wants an end piece, or keep it for yourself. Take it out of this world and beyond and eat with Mitts-Full MUFU sauce (page 46).

MUSHROOM MEATBALLS

For meatballs, I find ground turkey is one of the most flavorful ways to go, especially with a bit of pork thrown in the mix. This recipe, like the ragù on page 112, makes good use of the simple, essential box grater. By grating and sautéing the mushrooms and onion, you can give even tired meat the spirit and color it needs for success.

Very nice atop a spoonful of Winter Squash Sauce (page 128).

MAKES 6 SERVINGS

2 cups fresh or 1 cup dried bread crumbs, plus more as needed

⅓ cup whole milk, plus more as needed

1 medium yellow onion, peeled

12 ounces large button mushrooms

2 tablespoons cooking oil, olive or vegetable, plus more as needed (see Tips, page 7)

Fine sea salt or kosher salt

1 pound ground turkey (see Tips, page 10)

½ pound ground pork (see Tips, page 10)

Ground black pepper

2 eggs

2 garlic cloves, pounded with a pinch of salt (see Tips, page 7)

2 tablespoons chopped fresh parsley leaves

2 tablespoons chopped fresh mint leaves or ½ teaspoon dried mint

½ cup grated Parmesan or Grana Padano cheese

2 cups tomato sauce (optional)

1½ pounds pasta (optional)

In a medium bowl, combine the bread crumbs and milk and set aside to soak. (Have some extra bread crumbs on hand in case you need to adjust the meatball mixture later.) **Using** the large holes of a box grater, grate the onion and the mushrooms. Heat a large skillet (see Tips, page 6) over high heat, add the oil, then add the onion and mushrooms and ½ teaspoon salt. Cook, stirring occasionally, until the liquid from the onion and mushrooms has evaporated, about 10 minutes. Set aside to cool completely.

Meanwhile, in a large bowl, combine the ground meats with ¾ teaspoon salt, grinds of black pepper, eggs, garlic, parsley, mint, and cheese. Squeeze any excess liquid from the bread crumbs and add them and the cooled mushroom mixture to the bowl. Use your hands to mix well, squeezing the meatball mixture through your fingers so that everything is well distributed, but remember that overhandling ground meat can make it turn tough, so don't. If the mixture seems too wet—ground turkey is often quite moist—add some dry bread crumbs.

Heat a large skillet over medium heat. Make a small "taster" patty and fry it in a little oil on both sides until cooked through. Taste it and adjust for salt and texture—if the mixture seems too wet, mix in some more bread crumbs; too dry, a little splash of milk.

Use your hands to form the mixture into Ping-Pong–size balls. Refrigerate if not cooking soon.

Reheat the skillet over medium heat, add a tablespoon or two of oil and then the meatballs, starting at one side and working to the other. As they brown, turn them in the order they went in. Turn and brown three or four times, adjusting the heat as needed so that they cook through without burning. Break one open to check for doneness.

If you're planning to eat the meatballs with tomato sauce and pasta, add your sauce, or just some chopped tomatoes, to the skillet and let it all simmer while you boil the pasta in salted water. Add a splash of water to the skillet if needed to keep it saucy.

Also

- Mushroom Meatballs are great in a hot sandwich with tomato sauce and melted mozzarella or provolone cheese.
- Make them smaller (walnut-size), sprinkle with grated cheese or chopped herbs, and serve as an appetizer.
- Meatballs freeze well too, cooked or raw.

SPECIAL SAUCES FOR THE BORING

A little bad taste is like a nice splash
of paprika. We all need a splash of bad
taste—it's hearty, it's healthy, it's physical.
I think we could use *more* of it. *No* taste is
what I'm against.

—DIANA VREELAND

I stand firmly with Ms. Vreeland against no taste. Nevertheless, it happens, and can be a source of inspiration. When food is boring, that's when we need sauce. I'm with Lady Macbeth too: "From thence, the sauce to meat is ceremony; Meeting were bare without it." Splashing these sauces around brings flair to the bare.

VEGETABLE PUREES

When our eldest, Hop, was a baby, we resolved to bubble up out of the murk of jarred purees and make our own. We found a clever device for doing just that: the Happy Baby Grinder, a name far too Grimm for us, so we called it the Mini-Mill. It was a simple three-piece setup into which nearly any food could be loaded. You topped it with the grinder plate, and with a twist up, out would squirm worms of baby food! We took it everywhere, asking for demitasse spoons and quietly milling bites of our entrées at restaurants, and making potluck purees at parties.

It wasn't long before chef-daddy found other kitchen uses for the Mini-Mill as well. At first I used it to grind up cooked onions or leeks or fennel to add to other sauces but soon found that I could spin up a portion of vegetables that I was cooking as a side, add oil or butter, and use the resulting purees as a sauce to spread under the meat. Dry-ish specimens were especially helped by this treatment, and sandwiches were made moist with a spread on their bread. Eventually I broke the first Mini-Mill by feeding it meat beyond its abilities (why was I pureeing meat?)

and permanently retired the second to non-baby use after a batch of roasted garlic left an unerasable memory.

You are sure to come up with your own concoctions using this same basic technique, but here are some that have spread successfully around our house. These recipes all begin with steamed or boiled, or over-steamed or -boiled, vegetables. Toss them and the suggested ingredients in your blender, food processor, or hand-cranked food mill (mini or otherwise). Add olive or vegetable oil for richness and just enough water to make it smooth.

Carrots with Saffron or Cinnamon:
Add some onions cooked to soft sweetness if the carrots need extra help. Nice with Spice-Encrusted BS Chicken Breast Roast (page 116) or on a sandwich with spreadable cheese. Add spoonfuls of yogurt and it's a dip for bread or raw vegetables.

Cauliflower with Lemon and Turmeric:
Add some onions cooked to soft sweetness if the cauliflower needs extra help. Delicious with BS Chicken Breast,

Tangy and Turmerical (page 115); or as a good bed for lamb or fish; or for roasted cabbage, Brussels sprouts, or . . . more cauliflower!

Broccoli with Parsley, Feta, and Black Pepper: I once spread this on a toast before I put a fried egg on it. That was a good morning. My son Liam and I agree that it's delicious on a turkey sandwich, though it's true that I lay it on thicker.

Green Beans with Fig and Balsamic Vinegar: Tends to be not the prettiest puree, so hide it under BS Chicken Breast, Dorato-Style (page 114) or slices of pork. Or let appearances be damned and thickly spride (spread with pride) on rustic toasts, then crumble over a mild cheese like ricotta or ricotta salata.

Brussels Sprouts with Orange, Ginger, and Brown Butter: Can stand up, and stand up to, any meat. Use orange zest and squeeze in some of the juice. Good with Chipotle Chicken Thighs with Cumin and Honey (page 110).

Peas with Sage and Mint, or with Cumin and Coriander: First time I had mushy peas I was as hooked as the cod that had been fried and set atop them. Pea puree elegantly rescues overdone lamb and makes a pretty, pale tendril-colored dip when chickpeas are blended in.

Winter Squash with Cardamom: Overcooked winter squash is not really a problem that needs fixing; I just love this puree so much I had to include it. Butter, melted or browned, can be used instead of oil for an especially rich feeling. So good with Mushroom Meatballs (page 121) and makes a great breakfast or lunch with a poached egg and a spattering of hot sauce, like harissa.

SMASHED BEANS

To answer your first question: Yes, we're talking about bean puree—*smashed beans* just sounds better. Second, smashed beans are a sauce? I know. But if you think about hummus, or frijoles refritos, and how they are kind of saucy, you'll start picking up what I'm laying down. And where I'm laying it, like under those overroasted vegetables (page 18) or crunchy salad greens, tangily dressed. Or under slices, whatever their cooked-ness, of pork, chop or roast, or sausage or bacon. (Even, especially perhaps, bologna could use the help; never much of a cold-cuts-sandwich guy, I opt for quick-frying sliced meats and eating them with some smashed-up beans, leaves of cilantro or lettuce, maybe a couple of tortillas. Mostly this happens when I am not the one doing the shopping, like when I'm visiting, but when I do buy prepared meats, I make sure to find organic bologna, hot dogs, ham.) Or I just roll the beans, lettuce, and cilantro in warm tortillas and leave it like that.

Smashed beans can also support: eggs any style, salads and slaws, sliced tomatoes and cucumbers, and, of course, bread, crackers, or chips. Also, whatever you want.

Follow the MUFU recipes in Can of Beans, page 45. Spin the results in the blender or food processor until smooth. If needed, add just enough of the reserved liquid to make pureeing happen—too much liquid will make the smashed beans taste washed out.

The Mitts-Full MUFU: Can of Corn and Can of Black Beans (page 46): Do not be put off by the pond-mud appearance and just go ahead and spread this Mitts-Full MUFU smash under a couple of fried eggs and shake on hot sauce. Or, before your next barbecue, like the day before, make a batch. Refrigerate it and when somebody's cousin burns the chicken? Heat it up and rescue them. Also, blow your own mind and have a full-on flavor party with Hot-Patootie Meatloaf (page 120)!

The Garbonanza MUFU: Chickpea with Turmeric and Cilantro (page 48): Spread under Roasted Vegetable Salad with Ginger, Lime, and Sour Cream (page 20) but skip the sour cream. Spread under chicken cooked any way, including fried, or with Gluten-Free Not-Rings (page 89).

White Bean MUFU: Tuscan Style (page 47): With pork, on toast, a bacon sandwich, a tomato sandwich, a mushroom sandwich, a greens sandwich, a salad sandwich.

Red Bean MUFU: Smoky Style (page 50): Spread this on your hot dog bun! Put under shrimps as if it were grits! Make arrangements involving avocado slices and tortillas. Dip Skaket Beach Thins (page 87) in it. Eat with Tortilla Española on Vacation (page 60).

NUT SALSAS AND SAUCES

Toast and chop some nuts and mix with garlic, chopped herbs or ground spices, and olive oil and you've made a tasty salsa with a little heft that's good on most things. There are *so* many possible combinations; I'll just list a few favorites to prime the pump.

But first, for a few general tips about toasting nuts and using raw garlic, see Tips, pages 7 and 8.

Also:

- Use good olive oil for salsas, or a neutral oil if you don't have that.
- Salt the salsa lightly at first—it can be easy to overdo it.
- Citrus juices and vinegars, if using, should be added to herby salsas right before serving so they don't muddy the color.
- Nut salsas and sauces keep well for a couple of days, tightly covered and refrigerated.

Hazelnut, parsley, sage, and orange:
Garlic or no garlic; finely chop or grate orange zest or thinly slice some kumquats (discard any seeds you may find). **Uses:** with BS Chicken Breast, Dorato-Style (page 114); a natural with pork or duck; as an accompaniment to a cheese board; on toasts with cream cheese.

Almond, parsley, mint, and scallion:
Squeeze some lemon juice on the chopped scallions before mixing in; garlic or not. **Uses:** serve with Spice-Encrusted BS Chicken Breast Roast (page 116);

spoon over fish or lamb; toss with boiled vegetables, like green beans, turnips, or asparagus; toss with roasted vegetables, like cauliflower, carrots, or beets.

Peanut, cilantro, scallion, and chile:
Squeeze some lime juice on the chopped scallions before mixing in. Use diced jalapeño or other fresh chile; dried ground sweet red chiles like Marash, Urfa, or Aleppo; or prepared chile paste like sambal oelek; garlic. **Uses:** pass at the table with Vindaloo-Style Pork Etcetrazzini (page 26); dress rice noodles and vegetables; dress sliced cucumbers and tomatoes; spoon over cool silken tofu or hot fried or steamed firm tofu; pass a bowl at the table to sauce stir-fries.

Walnut, rosemary, fennel seed, and black pepper: With chopped parsley; garlic; crushed red pepper flakes; balsamic vinegar. **Uses:** lambilicious, especially with Lamb Leg Etcetrazzini (page 28); with goat cheese; spoon over hot boiled potatoes and lean into the aromatic reminiscences.

Pecan, celery, thyme, and tarragon:
Dice and quickly boil the celery till crisp-tender; lemon zest. **Uses:** with grilled chicken that's spicy with red and black pepper; with BS Chicken Breast, Tangy and Turmerical (page 115); spoon over halved boiled eggs and/or boiled little potatoes.

Pistachio, cilantro or parsley, and coriander: Garlic or not; citrus zest—try grapefruit! **Uses:** spoon over peeled and sliced grapefruits or oranges and scoops of avocado; over shrimp or chicken cooked any way; over grilled or roasted eggplant or zucchini; dress raw shredded cabbage, carrots, turnips, and/or radishes for the best slaw (add salt and extra acidity— citrus juices, rice vinegar); on pasta (skip the citrus and add Parmesan or, arguably better, queso fresco or ricotta salata).

Cashew, cumin seed, brown butter, and hot pepper: Garlic or not. Here, butter (page 143) replaces oil and if it cools, this salsa goes solid, so keep warm. **Uses:** with Spice-Encrusted BS Chicken Breast Roast (page 116); spoon onto hot boiled cauliflower or broccoli florets, cabbage wedges, carrots slices, snap peas; spoon into baked potatoes; on popcorn.

YOGURT SAUCES

Yogurt sauces are easy to whirl up smooth in a blender but also can be stirred up in a bowl and left a little chunky. These suggestions are good as they are, or with olive oil mixed in, and they will all need pinches of salt.

These are every one of them good with fish, chicken, and lamb; dolloped onto bowls of warm or cool chickpeas or lentils; swooshed onto bowls of smooth vegetable soup; spread on sandwiches; spooned over grilled or roasted vegetables; zigzagged over hot boiled asparagus, green beans, or cauliflower; used as a dressing for romaine, iceberg, or radicchio salads; swirled over tomato, cucumber, sweet pepper, or beet salads; dipped up with raw vegetables or pita.

Mix into plain whole-milk yogurt:

- garlic, lots of parsley, and lemon juice
- garlic, grated cucumber, and mint
- garlic and red chiles like Marash, Urfa, or Aleppo, or prepared chile paste like sambal oelek
- grated fresh turmeric, ginger, cilantro, lime juice and zest
- cumin, nigella, and mustard seeds sizzled in a little oil
- dill, chives, sumac, and lemon juice

THE CREAM

Cream is good and wonderful, but just please be careful; I've seen it go a little out of control. I once knew, for example, a cocaine-dealing dishwasher who would drink the remains of the cream pitchers as they came back to the dish room. He kept his money in the toe of his shoe. He didn't look that healthy. I was told, by energetic waiters who seemed to know, that the coke was dry but the change was a little damp.

The upshot: cream in moderation, skip the coke, get yourself a wallet or a money belt or something.

Cream has a nice flavor itself, of course, but what we are mostly interested in here is cream's ability to *carry* flavor, to float it on a fatty little raft right to your taste buds. You may find different types of cream at your store: light, heavy, whipping. The difference has to do with the amount of milkfat—light has between 30 and 36 percent milkfat, heavy (a.k.a. whipping) has 36 to 40 percent. Higher milkfat content makes for slightly better results when whipping, but otherwise the types are interchangeable.

Whipped, cold, hot, sour, spicy, or sweet. Here we go.

PENNE IN PINK

Penne alla vodka is a blushing-pink creamy classic. Baffled as to why the vodka is there, I skip it and make Penne in Pink while I sip cold gin and consider what other pasta sauces could be fortified with cream.

MAKES 4 SERVINGS

Fine sea salt or kosher salt

2 tablespoons olive oil

2 tablespoons butter

1 yellow onion, diced

2 garlic cloves, finely chopped

Crushed red pepper flakes to taste

One 15-ounce can whole peeled tomatoes, chopped, their juices reserved separately

1 pound rigatoni or fettucine

¼ cup light or heavy cream (but not half-and-half; it will break)

Chopped fresh parsley leaves, as desired

Parmesan or Grana Padano cheese, for serving

Put a big pot of cold water on to boil. Add salt.

Meanwhile, heat a large skillet (see Tips, page 6) over high heat add the oil and butter, then the onion and ½ teaspoon salt. Stir until things get sizzling, then reduce the heat to medium and cook, stirring occasionally, until the onion is soft but not browned, about 15 minutes. Add the garlic and red pepper flakes, cook a minute more, and add the chopped tomatoes and a little more salt. Increase the heat to get the sauce bubbling, then lower to a simmer. Add the penne to the boiling salted water, and the sauce will be done when the penne is.

As the skillet gets to looking (and sounding) dry and sizzly, add doses of the reserved tomato juices. Stir in the cream, taste, adjust, and add the drained pasta (save ½ cup of the water) and the parsley. Toss to coat well, then taste once more before serving. Think especially about the texture of the sauce—it will continue to thicken as it cools and is absorbed by the pasta, so you will likely want to add a splash of the reserved pasta cooking water to keep it flowy.

Pass Parmesan or Grana Padano to sprinkle over at the table.

CREAMY CABBAGE WITH CARAWAY SEEDS, DILL, AND HOT PEPPER

When she's not making art, Kathleen has always been a gardener and educator. One year, she planted a type of collard green in the school garden that grew into a tree and just kept on giving. And giving. I felt like a jerk when I said the tree collards weren't, well, my favorite, then immediately set about finding a way to change that. Cooking them with onion, cream, and spices worked and works just as well with cabbage (if not better—sorry, Kath!).

MAKES 4 TO 6 SERVINGS

3 tablespoons cooking oil, olive or vegetable (see Tips, page 7)

1 yellow onion, diced

¾ teaspoon fine sea salt or kosher salt

½ teaspoon whole caraway seeds (see Tips, page 8)

2 tablespoons chopped dill leaves and tender stems (or cilantro, or both)

Crushed red pepper flakes

1 small or ½ large head of red, green, or Savoy cabbage, roughly sliced or chopped

½ cup light or heavy cream (but not half-and-half; it will break)

½ teaspoon red wine vinegar

Heat a large skillet (see Tips, page 6) over high heat and add the oil, then the onion and ½ teaspoon of the salt. Stir until it gets going, then reduce the heat to medium and cook, stirring occasionally, until the onion is softened, but not entirely, 8 to 10 minutes. Add the caraway seeds, dill, and a fun pinch of red pepper flakes and stir for 30 seconds. Add the cabbage, remaining ¼ teaspoon salt, and 1 cup water. Cover and cook, stirring occasionally and adding splashes of water if needed to keep it stewy, for 10 minutes.

Uncover, add the cream, and cook until the cabbage is tender, 5 to 10 minutes. The cabbage should be saucy but not soupy—add water if too dry, continue cooking if too wet. Stir in the vinegar, taste, adjust, and serve now or reheat, with a splash of water, when ready. Very good alongside Dijon Chicken Thighs Royale (page 107) or BS Chicken Breast, Easy-Fried Two Ways (pages 113), or Spice-Encrusted BS Chicken Breast Roast (page 116).

CREAMY SWEET PEPPERS WITH SEEDS NOT THEIR OWN

Colorful alongside green lentils, green beans, green salad, or greens. Nice tossed with farfalle, actually, or with rice.

MAKES 4 TO 6 SERVINGS

¼ cup cooking oil, olive or vegetable (see Tips, page 7), plus a little more

1 medium yellow onion, thinly sliced

2 large yellow, orange, or red bell peppers (1 pound), halved, stemmed, seeds and stuff removed, and thinly sliced

1 teaspoon fine sea salt or kosher salt

1 teaspoon yellow, brown, and/or black mustard seeds

1 teaspoon nigella seeds (if not available, substitute cumin seeds)

2 garlic cloves, finely chopped or thinly sliced

3 tablespoons chopped fresh cilantro leaves and tender stems (optional)

3 tablespoons toasted sesame seeds (see Tips, page 8)

½ cup light or heavy cream (but not half-and-half; it will break)

1 tablespoon red wine vinegar or other vinegar that isn't balsamic

Heat a large skillet (see Tips, page 6) over high heat. Add the oil, then right away the onion and peppers. Add the salt, mustard seeds, and nigella seeds and stir. Reduce the heat to medium and cook, stirring occasionally, until the peppers and onion are tender and melty, about 20 minutes. Add a splash of water as needed to keep the skillet juicy.

Move the peppers and onion to one side of the skillet, add a little more oil if needed, and add the garlic and cilantro, if using, to sizzle in the clearing. Stir until the cilantro wilts and the garlic smells very good, about 20 seconds, then add the sesame seeds, cream, and vinegar and stir everything together. Simmer for a few minutes, adding water if needed to keep some flow.

DIP OF FOOLS

Do this: For a simple dessert for four people, put ½ cup cold cream in a bowl with ½ teaspoon granulated sugar and whip till whipped, then stir in one (or more, in separate bowls) of the following flavorants. Sit around like happy fools dipping stuff in it—cookies, biscuits, cake, slices of fruit, fingers.

- a teaspoon of finely ground coffee
- a tablespoon or two of finely ground nuts (see Tips, page 8)
- a tablespoon of cocoa and a pinch of cinnamon
- grated chocolate to taste
- a tablespoon of maple syrup (skip the granulated sugar)
- a tablespoon of jam or jelly (skip the granulated sugar)

BUTTER

The father of my Italian friend Gianno was a farm inspector, and he gave me my first ever taste of olive oil. My good/bad luck: It was primo olio nuovo from the legendary hills of Lucca, pressed earlier that day. Like centuries of eaters before me, I was spellbound for life. Green liquid oil from a hard-gnarled tree. How could it be so rich and bright, fruit-fragrant and pepper-hot? It's a fat, but it's almost a drink. It felt like destiny, and I brought tins of it home with me, bestowing it around and being baffled by the palate-shrug it was sometimes greeted with. Maybe it only works in Lucca, I wondered, the way a pew's just a bench when it's not in church. Or maybe it was the ubiquity and dominance of butter in American kitchens.

Native Lucchese probably don't remember their first ever taste of the best olive oil in the world, just as I don't remember my first ever taste of butter. We were babies, Americans brought up buttered, and not having little epiphanies over what was smeared on our slices of Wonder.

Even though I don't have the same kind of gob-smacked, lightning-struck, first-contact butter lore like I have for olive oil, I like butter, I do. Here's what's great about butter: it comes from the sun by way of grass by way of peacefully grazing cows; it reveals a range of flavors determined by temperature, from sweet cold to nutty hot; it's a semi-solid emulsion that can hold all kinds of flavors in its embrace and then deliver them with a gentle, melting grace; just like olive oil, it's great straight, on hot vegetables, on potatoes, and lavished on our old friend toast.

BROWN BUTTERS

Brown butter is like pale, creamy pan sauce's nutty, greasy, burnout brother who, upon closer inspection, turns out to be elegant and rich.

In a small skillet over medium-high heat, melt 1 tablespoon of butter per serving. It'll foam, subside, grow ominously still, then smoke slightly, and the little bits at the bottom will brown. Carefully taste a little to see if it's the way you like it.

- Toss in some roughly chopped sage leaves, let them sizzle and use to stir into sautéed corn, boiled green beans, asparagus, or snap peas, or to spoon over grilled or roasted eggplant or mushrooms, fish, or sliced pork.

- Toss in some toasted and chopped nuts—hazelnuts, walnuts, almonds, pistachios—and use as above, also over goat cheese on toast, or on boiled cauliflower, turnips, snap peas, or green beans.
- Add ground spices like cumin, coriander (see Tips, page 8), and crushed red pepper flakes to use as above and over boiled potatoes, rice, or on grilled or roasted chicken.
- Use to top scrambled eggs.
- Mix with toasted sesame seeds (see Tips, page 8) for popcorn.
- Use in Hackaroni and Cheese (page 43).

BUTTER PAN SAUCE

If you swirl pats of cold butter with a little liquid in a hot-ish pan, a creamy sauce forms. The why of it is science, and when I look it up for some understanding and am faced with . . .

. . . I decide that I don't really need to know why it works, just that it is delicious. And I'm reminded, not unpleasantly, why my job at the chemistry lab would be to make fancy, buttery lunches for the smart scientists.

MAKES 4 SERVINGS

¼ cup white wine (or red or rosé)

4 tablespoons (½ stick) butter, cold and cut into 4 slices

Fine sea salt or kosher salt

Lemon juice, white wine vinegar, cider vinegar, or red wine vinegar

Chopped fresh herbs, like chives, chervil, mint, parsley, or thyme (optional)

Ideally, the pan you cooked your fish, meat, or mushrooms in has brown, but not black, flavorful bits stuck to it and is ready to be deglazed with liquid before the butter goes in. If not, or if you're using a clean pan, that's fine too. Add the wine to the skillet and reduce over medium heat, using a wooden spoon to scrape up any glazy leavings. When the wine is thickened and nearly syrupy, about 2 minutes, reduce the heat to very low and add the butter, swirling and stirring to melt and emulsify it. If it is bubbling hard and begins to look more greasy than creamy, splash in a little water. Taste for salt and add a squeeze of lemon or drops of vinegar as needed. Stir in the herbs, if using, and spoon over your stuff.

COMPOUND BUTTERS

Compound butter is butter mixed with flavorful ingredients. Simple stuff, melting wherever help is needed, a dollop packing a welcome wallop. Of course you should go wild with it, come up with all kinds of compound combos and places to put them, but I will suggest a few of my favorites for each type.

Making compound butter is difficult if not impossible with cold, hard butter and super-easy with softened, you-could-easily-squish-a-stick-with-your-fingers butter. These recipes all start with a quarter-pound of the latter, which will likely be more than you need:

a good thing because compound butter can be formed into logs, wrapped in plastic or parchment paper, and frozen. Very handy to be able to slice off some rounds when you need them.

The method is the same for all these recipes: Put 1 stick softened unsalted butter in a medium bowl or the bowl of a food processor and mix with the specified ingredients below until completely combined. Only a few of these butters have garlic listed, but it would be good in any of them, with the possible exception of the citrus butter.

HERB BUTTER

On fish, baked or boiled potatoes, chicken breasts; melting atop smooth vegetable soup, or any soup.

½ cup (1 stick) unsalted butter, softened

⅓ to ½ cup finely chopped fresh parsley, cilantro, basil, mint, tarragon (use just a tablespoon, with the rest parsley), chervil, chives, or a combination

¼ teaspoon fine sea salt or kosher salt

GREEN GARLIC BUTTER

On toasted bread, of course. Also, on all meats (including a hamburger), all vegetables, scrambled eggs, beans.

½ cup (1 stick) unsalted butter, softened

2 (or more) garlic cloves, finely grated or pounded to a paste (see Tips, page 7)

¼ cup finely chopped fresh parsley

2 tablespoons grated Parmesan or Grana Padano cheese

Pinch of crushed red pepper flakes

¼ teaspoon fine sea salt or kosher salt

GOLDEN SPICED BUTTER

On rice, of course. Also, on chicken, fish, lamb, green beans, cauliflower, carrots, corn (kernels or on-the-cob), peas, lentils. Stir into scrambled eggs, especially if you need the cure to last night's excesses.

½ cup (1 stick) unsalted butter, softened

1 tablespoon ground cumin (see Tips, page 8)

1 tablespoon ground coriander (see Tips, page 8)

2 teaspoons ground turmeric

2 teaspoons paprika

1 teaspoon ground fennel (see Tips, page 8)

Cayenne or other hot pepper to taste

¼ teaspoon fine sea salt or kosher salt

Grated zest of ½ lime (optional)

Juice of 1 lime (optional)

ANCHOVY BUTTER

On all meats, in omelets, or atop scrambled eggs, broccoli, chickpeas.

½ cup (1 stick) unsalted butter, softened

One 4-ounce can anchovy fillets, drained

1 garlic clove, finely grated or pounded to a paste (see Tips, page 7)

2 tablespoons finely chopped fresh parsley

1½ teaspoons finely chopped fresh marjoram or ½ teaspoon dried oregano (optional)

Ground black pepper

¼ teaspoon fine sea salt or kosher salt

CAPER-LEMON BUTTER

On fish, chicken breasts, pork chops, boiled potatoes, asparagus, green beans, carrots.

½ cup (1 stick) unsalted butter, softened

⅓ cup drained capers

2 tablespoons finely chopped fresh parsley

1 teaspoon finely chopped fresh marjoram or ½ teaspoon dried oregano (optional)

Grated zest of ½ lemon (optional)

Juice of 1 lemon (optional)

¼ teaspoon fine sea salt or kosher salt

GINGER BUTTER

On pork or chicken, roasted beets or other root vegetables; stirred into lentils.

½ cup (1 stick) unsalted butter, softened

2 inches of fresh ginger, grated (about 2 tablespoons)

1 tablespoon ground coriander (see Tips, page 8)

1 teaspoon grated lemon zest

CITRUS BUTTER

On fish, chicken; melted atop smooth vegetable soup, or any soup.

½ cup (1 stick) unsalted butter, softened

2 tablespoons grated lemon, lime, orange, grapefruit zests in any combination (if using lime only, start with 1 tablespoon—it can get bitter in larger quantities)

2 tablespoons juice of whichever citrus you're using

¼ teaspoon fine sea salt or kosher salt

CHILE-LIME BUTTER

On corn especially. Also, on roasted cabbage or Brussels sprouts, grilled vegetables, steaks, or pork chops.

½ cup (1 stick) unsalted butter, softened

¼ cup sweet ground chile (in Korean grocery stores, jars of mild, bright red coarsely ground chiles can be found that are more

flavorful than most powdered chiles)

Zest and juice of 1 or more limes

¼ teaspoon fine sea salt or kosher salt

CODA: A COLLECTION OF DRINKS TO FORGET YOU BY

We go down the hall again,
thank heaven, to my drink.
—JAMES BALDWIN, *GIOVANNI'S ROOM*

In early 2019, I started doing something stupid. I mean, I'd done stupid things before, I'm sure, but this time I was opening my own restaurant. By the end of the year I was broke and nearly broken. We limped through the gray early months of 2020, our handsome, spacious dining rooms nowhere near full enough. We were seeing a glimmer of spring light when the pandemic struck and doused it. Later, sweeping floors and selling equipment, we laughed when we heard restaurant reopening guidelines announcing that places with a 100-person capacity would be serving just 10 guests instead; we'd been ahead of our time. *sob*

It wasn't all bad, though, and the best thing was getting to work with the people who eventually made up our great staff. But before we found that sweet and brilliant bunch, there were a few interviews that went sour. The (eventually) funniest of them served as inspiration for a series of after-dinner drinks meant to settle the stomach and mind, if not the score.

I'd posted that we were hiring line cooks. Looking back, I see a row of fluttering flags, red as cherries, but at the time I thought First Interview was . . . okay. We really needed some staff, and I was feeling, if not generous, then at least less than cynical. The very next morning, First Interview texted to explain that they had another interview that day, should they go, or . . . ? I hadn't made any staffing decisions, was still interviewing, and responded that First Interview should go ahead with their plans, I'd be in touch. Thank you, I added and then actually gasped when the three dots turned into a bubble that yelled, "All right, fuck you too, old man!" Done gasping, I winced. I went to the mirror to see *how* old, and winced again. Then I started laughing and looked much better. That night, I came up with the first of the Old Man drinks and felt better still.

BITTER OLD MAN

1½ ounces bitters (ideally Varnelli Amaro Dell'Erborista)
1½ ounces brandy
1 cold, cold cube of ice (optional)

Mix in a glass. Add ice for a Cold & Bitter Old Man.

CRAZY OLD MAN

1½ ounces absinthe
1½ ounces brandy

Mix in a glass.

ELDERLY OLD MAN

1 ounce elderflower liqueur
2 ounces brandy

Mix in a glass.

RED-FACED OLD MAN

1 ounce Cappelletti aperitif
2 ounces brandy
1 cold, cold cube of ice (optional)

Mix in a glass. Add ice for a Cold Red-Faced Old Man.

SWEET OLD MAN

1 ounce anisette
2 ounces brandy

Mix in a glass.

SOUR OLD MAN

1 ounce tart umeshu plum liqueur
2 ounces brandy

Mix in a glass.

FUCK YOU TOO OLD MAN

3 ounces brandy

1 joint

Pour the brandy into a glass. Balance the joint across the glass,
from rim to rim, like a bridge. Burn the bridge.

WISE OLD MAN

8 ounces bubbly water or water

Pour in a glass; drink all of it. Roar out a fierce, youthful belch. Go to bed.

ACKNOWLEDGMENTS

Many thanks to:

Liam Peternell, for taking photos between high school classes and eating the subjects for lunch.

Milo Henderson, for his creative, infectious love of snacks.

Hop Peternell, for their good cooking and great advice.

Kathleen Henderson, for cups of mint tea, skillets of garlicky broccoli, and a really comfortable mask covered in daisies.

Liam, Milo, Hop, and Kathleen, for all your help at The Lede—I literally would not have survived without you.

Mom and Dad, for so much, including my virgin voyage to Walmart.

Johanna Heine, Anne Marxer, and Chris Heine, for the funny games and dinner poddies that got us through The Year.

The farm workers, truck drivers, dock workers, grocery store workers, sanitation workers, and everyone else who helped to keep us cooking and fed during the most trying of times—you sustain us and have all my gratitude!

Hudson Ranch & Vineyards, San Francisco Cooking School, and Ene Osteraas-Constable and Scott Constable at Wowhaus for generously providing quiet places to write.

The guys at San Quentin State Prison, for reminding me how much we need flavor and for being the best students at the hardest cooking school.

Sharon Bowers, for her continued guidance and quarantine giggles.

Cassie Jones and Jill Zimmerman, for their assurance and reassurances—I needed them.

Everyone else at William Morrow, especially Liate Stehlik, Ben Steinberg, Anna Brill, Alison Hinchcliffe, Mumtaz Mustafa, Rachel Meyers, Renata De Oliveira, and Anna Brower.

UNIVERSAL CONVERSION CHART

Oven temperature equivalents

250°F = 120°C

275°F = 135°C

300°F = 150°C

325°F = 160°C

350°F = 180°C

375°F = 190°C

400°F = 200°C

425°F = 220°C

450°F = 230°C

475°F = 240°C

500°F = 260°C

Measurement equivalents

Measurements should always be level unless directed otherwise.

⅛ teaspoon = 0.5 mL

¼ teaspoon = 1 mL

½ teaspoon = 2 mL

1 teaspoon = 5 mL

1 tablespoon = 3 teaspoons = ½ fluid ounce = 15 mL

2 tablespoons = ⅛ cup = 1 fluid ounce = 30 mL

4 tablespoons = ¼ cup = 2 fluid ounces = 60 mL

5⅓ tablespoons = ⅓ cup = 3 fluid ounces = 80 mL

8 tablespoons = ½ cup = 4 fluid ounces = 120 mL

10⅔ tablespoons = ⅔ cup = 5 fluid ounces = 160 mL

12 tablespoons = ¾ cup = 6 fluid ounces = 180 mL

16 tablespoons = 1 cup = 8 fluid ounces = 240 mL

INDEX

NOTE: PAGE REFERENCES IN *ITALICS* REFER TO PHOTOS.

A

alcoholic beverages. *see* drinks
anchovies
    Anchovy Butter, 147
    in Caesar Salad Dressing, 72
    Cannellini Bean and Celery Salad with
        Anchovies, 51
    Sardine and Anchovy S'cool, about, 54
    Spaghetti with Cream, Garlic, and Anchovies,
        55
Arugula Almond Not-Pesto, 75

B

bacon, pork, and sausage
    Celery Baked with Black Pepper, Bacon, and
        Cream, 92, 93
    Mac and Peas (and bacon), 44
    pork in Gravy, 118–119
    sausage in Nachos with Queso Fundido
        (Molten Cheese), 65
    Vindaloo-Style Pork Etcetrazzini, 26–28
Baked Potatoes and Surrogate Fries, 103
beans
    Cannellini Bean and Celery Salad with
        Anchovies, 51
    Can of Beans Cooked with Rice and Lots of
        Scallions and Cilantro, 52
    Chickpeas with Tomato, Rosemary, and
        Cream, 53
    mash-up fry-ups (MUFUs), about, 45
    Milo's Bean Dip, 68, 69
    The Mitts-Full MUFU: Can of Corn *and* Can
        of Black Beans, 46
    in My Cakes, Nacho Cakes, 66, 67
    Red Bean MUFU: Smoky Style, 50
    Smashed Beans, 129
    White Bean MUFU: Tuscan Style, 47
Beef Jerky and Spinach Hackaroni and Cheese, 44
beverages. *see* drinks
Bitter Old Man, 153

bread
    bread crumbs, 9
    Burnt Toast, 14, *15*
    Cheesy Onion Bread Pudding, 17
    croutons, 9
    Onion Panade, *13*, 16
broccoli
    Broccoli with Parsley, Feta, and Black Pepper,
        pureed, 128
    Brocco Tacos, 83–84
Brown Butter, Brussels Sprouts with Orange, Ginger
    (pureed), 128
Brown Butters, 143
Brussels Sprouts with Orange, Ginger, and Brown
    Butter, pureed, 128
BS Chicken Breast. *see also* chicken, boneless
    skinless
    Dorato-Style, 114
    Easy-Fried Two Ways, about, 113
    Roast, Spice-Encrusted, 116
    Tangy and Turmerical, 115
BS Chicken Thighs, about, 106
burnt and overcooked foods, 13–33
    about, 14
    Burnt Toast, 14
    Cheesy Onion Bread Pudding, 17
    Coconut Rice Pudding with Ginger, 30
    Mushy Rice, 29
    Mushy Rice Pancakes, 31, *32–33*
    Onion Panade, *13*, 16
    Really Boiled Vegetables, 23
    Really Roasted Vegetables, about, 18
    Really Well-Done Meats, about, 24
    Roasted Vegetable Cornmeal Cakes, 19
    Roasted Vegetable Salad with Figgy Dressing,
        22
    Roasted Vegetable Salad with Ginger, Lime,
        and Sour Cream, 20, *21*
    Turkey Etcetrazzini and variations, 25–28,
        27

butter. *see also* compound butters; sauces and dips
about, 142
Brown Butters, 143
Brussels Sprouts with Orange, Ginger, and
Brown Butter, pureed, 128
Butter Pan Sauce, 144

C

Cabbage with Caraway Seeds, Dill, and Hot Pepper,
Creamy, 138, *139*
Caesar Salad Dressing, 72
canned beans. *see* mash-up fry-ups
Cannellini Bean and Celery Salad with Anchovies,
51
Can of Beans Cooked with Rice and Lots of
Scallions and Cilantro, 52
Caper-Lemon Butter, 148
carrots
Carrots Roasted in the Aftermath, *98*, 99
Carrots with Saffron or Cinnamon, pureed,
126
Glazed Carrot Phalanges (A.K.A. Baby
Carrots), *96*, 97
Cauliflower, Apple, Peas, and Spices, Vegetable
Soup with, *41*, 41–42
Cauliflower with Lemon and Turmeric, pureed,
126–128
celery
Baked with Black Pepper, Bacon, and Cream,
92, 93
Cannellini Bean and Celery Salad with
Anchovies, 51
Swooshes with Peanuts and Ginger, 90
cheese
Broccoli with Parsley, Feta, and Black Pepper,
pureed, 128
Cheesy Chicken Etcetrazzini, 26
Cheesy Onion Bread Pudding, 17
Creamy Chicken Ragù: Cheese Grater Edition,
112
Hackaroni and Cheese, 43–44
Nachos with Queso Fundido (Molten
Cheese), 65
Parmesan and Grana Padano, about, 11
chermoula sauce, in Carrots Roasted in the
Aftermath, *98*, 99

chicken, boneless skinless
BS Chicken Breast, Dorato-Style, 114
BS Chicken Breast, Easy-Fried Two Ways,
about, 113
BS Chicken Breast, Tangy and Turmerical, 115
BS Chicken Thighs, about, 106
Cheesy Chicken Etcetrazzini, 26
Chipotle Chicken Thighs with Cumin and
Honey, 110–111
Creamy Chicken Ragù: Cheese Grater Edition,
112
Dijon Chicken Thighs Royale, 107–109, *108*
Spice-Encrusted BS Chicken Breast Roast, 116
chickpeas
The Garbonanza MUFU: Chickpea with
Turmeric and Cilantro, 48, *49*
with Tomato, Rosemary, and Cream, 53
Chile-Lime Butter, 149
Chiles, Lime, and Fish Sauce, Roasted Radishes with,
94, 95
Chipotle Chicken Thighs with Cumin and Honey,
110–111
cilantro
about, 7
Can of Beans Cooked with Rice and Lots of
Scallions and Cilantro, 52
Cilantro Peanut Not-Pesto, 76
Corn, Cilantro, and Lime Hackaroni and
Cheese, 44
The Garbonanza MUFU: Chickpea with
Turmeric and Cilantro, 48, *49*
citrus
Caper-Lemon Butter, 148
Chile-Lime Butter, 149
Citrus Butter, 149
orange in Nuts Salsas and Sauces, 130
Roasted Radishes with Chiles, Lime, and Fish
Sauce, *94*, 95
Coconut Rice Pudding with Ginger, 30
compound butters
about, 145
Anchovy Butter, 147
Caper-Lemon Butter, 148
Chile-Lime Butter, 149
Citrus Butter, 149
Ginger Butter, 148

Golden Spiced Butter, 147
Green Garlic Butter, 146
Herb Butter, 146
corn. *see also* nachos
    Corn, Cilantro, and Lime Hackaroni and
        Cheese, 44
    The Mitts-Full MUFU: Can of Corn *and* Can
        of Black Beans, 46
    popcorn, 38–39
    Roasted Vegetable Cornmeal Cakes, 19
    in Unthick Clam Chowder: New England
        Version, Diner Version, 78–79
Crazy Old Man, 153
cream
    about, 136
    Creamy Cabbage with Caraway Seeds, Dill,
        and Hot Pepper, 138, *139*
    Creamy Chicken Ragù: Cheese Grater Edition,
        112
    Creamy Sweet Peppers with Seeds Not Their
        Own, *140*, 141
    in Penne in Pink, 137
croutons, about, 9

D

Dijon Chicken Thighs Royale, 107–109, *108*
Dip of Fools, 142
dressings. *see also* sauces and dips
    about, 70
    Caesar Salad Dressing, 72
    Figgy Dressing, 22
    Ranch Dressing, 71
drinks, 151–155
    about, 152
    Bitter Old Man, 153
    Crazy Old Man, 153
    Fuck You Too Old Man, 155
    Red-Faced Old Man, 154
    Sour Old Man, 154
    Sweet Old Man, 154
    Wise Old Man, 155

E

eggs
    about, 59
    in Mushy Rice, 29
    in Tortilla Española on Vacation, 60, *61*
enhanced dishes, 63–81
    Arugula Almond Not-Pesto, 75
    Caesar Salad Dressing, 72
    Cilantro Peanut Not-Pesto, 76
    dressings, about, 70
    Marjoram Walnut Not-Pesto, 74
    Milo's Bean Dip, 68, 69
    Mint Pistachio Not-Pesto, 77
    My Cakes, Nacho Cakes, 66, 67
    nachos, about, 64
    Nachos with Queso Fundido (Molten
        Cheese), 65
    Not-Pestos, 73
    Ranch Dressing, 71
    Unthick Clam Chowder: New England
        Version, Diner Version, 78–79
equipment essentials, 6
Etcetrazzini
    Cheesy Chicken, 26
    Herby Beef, 26
    Lamb Leg, 28
    Turkey, 25, 27
    Vindaloo-Style Pork, 26–28

F

Figgy Dressing, Roasted Vegetable Salad with, 22
fish. *see* anchovies; seafood
Fuck You Too Old Man, 155

G

The Garbonanza MUFU: Chickpea with Turmeric
    and Cilantro, 48, *49*
garlic. *see also* Not-Pestos
    about, 7
    in Caesar Salad Dressing, 72
    Green Garlic Butter, 146
    Spaghetti with Cream, Garlic, and Anchovies,
        55
ginger
    Brussels Sprouts with Orange, Ginger, and
        Brown Butter, pureed, 128
    Coconut Rice Pudding with Ginger, 30
    Ginger Butter, 148
    Roasted Vegetable Salad with Ginger, Lime,
        and Sour Cream, 20, *21*

ginger (*continued*)

Swooshes with Peanuts and Ginger, 90

Glazed Carrot Phalanges (A.K.A. Baby Carrots), *96*, 97

Gluten-Free Not-Rings, 89

Golden Spiced Butter, 147

Grana Padano, about, 11

Gravy, 118–119

Gravy, Meatloaf, and Meatballs, 117

Green Bean with Fig and Balsamic Vinegar, pureed, 128

Green Garlic Butter, 146

H

Hackaroni and Cheese, 43–44

hacking packages. *see* packaged foods

Hamburg-A-Roni: Campfire Edition, 57–58, *58*

herbs and spices. *see also* cilantro; garlic; ginger; Not-Pestos; turmeric

about, 7–8

Broccoli with Parsley, Feta, and Black Pepper, pureed, 128

Chickpeas with Tomato, Rosemary, and Cream, 53

Chipotle Chicken Thighs with Cumin and Honey, 110–111

Golden Spiced Butter, 147

Herb Butter, 146

Herby Beef Etcetrazzini, 26

Mushrooms with Honey and Coriander, 91

in Nut Salsas and Sauces, 130–134, *131–133*

Peas with Sage and Mint, or with Cumin and Coriander, pureed, 128

Spice-Encrusted BS Chicken Breast Roast, 116

Vegetable Soup with Cauliflower, Apple, Peas, and Spices, *41*, 41–42

honey

Chipotle Chicken Thighs with Cumin and Honey, 110–111

Mushrooms with Honey and Coriander, 91

Hot-Patootie Meatloaf, 120

I

ingredients, how to use them, 7–11

instant soup, 39–40

K

kitchen equipment essentials, 6

L

Lamb Leg Etcetrazzini, 28

limes

Chile-Lime Butter, 149

Roasted Radishes with Chiles, Lime, and Fish Sauce, 94, 95

Roasted Vegetable Salad with Ginger, Lime, and Sour Cream, 20, *21*

M

Mac and Peas (and bacon), 44

Marjoram Walnut Not-Pesto, 74

mash-up fry-ups (MUFUs)

about, 45

Can of Beans Cooked with Rice and Lots of Scallions and Cilantro, 52

Chickpeas with Tomato, Rosemary, and Cream, 53

The Garbonanza MUFU: Chickpea with Turmeric and Cilantro, 48, *49*

The Mitts-Full MUFU: Can of Corn *and* Can of Black Beans, 46

Red Bean MUFU: Smoky Style, 50

Smashed Beans, 129

White Bean MUFU: Tuscan Style, 47

meat, 105–123. *see also* bacon, pork, and sausage; chicken, boneless skinless; seafood

about, 10–11, 106

Beef Jerky and Spinach Hackaroni and Cheese, 44

BS Chicken Breast, Dorato-Style, 114

BS Chicken Breast, Easy-Fried Two Ways, about, 113

BS Chicken Breast, Tangy and Turmerical, 115

BS Chicken Thighs, about, 106

Chipotle Chicken Thighs with Cumin and Honey, 110–111

Creamy Chicken Ragù, 112

Dijon Chicken Thighs Royale, 107–109, *108*

Gravy, 118–119

Gravy, Meatloaf, and Meatballs, 117

Hamburg-A-Roni: Campfire Edition, 57–58, *58*

Herby Beef Etcetrazzini, 26

Hot-Patootie Meatloaf, 120
Lamb Leg Etcetrazzini, 28
Mushroom Meatballs, 121–123, *122*
Really Well-Done Meats, about, 24
Spice-Encrusted BS Chicken Breast Roast, 116
Mess of Scallions, *100,* 101
Milo's Bean Dip, 68, *69*
Mint Pistachio Not-Pesto, 77
Miso Hackaroni and Cheese, 43–44
mistakes, fixing, 2–3
The Mitts-Full MUFU: Can of Corn *and* Can of Black Beans, 46
Mushroom Meatballs, 121–123, *122*
Mushrooms with Honey and Coriander, 91
Mushy Rice, 29
Mushy Rice Pancakes, 31, *32–33*
My Cakes, Nacho Cakes, *66,* 67

N
nachos
    My Cakes, Nacho Cakes, *66,* 67
    Nachos, Two Ways, about, 64
    Nachos with Queso Fundido (Molten Cheese), 65
Not-Pestos, 73
    Arugula Almond, 75
    Cilantro Peanut, 76
    Marjoram Walnut, 74
    Mint Pistachio, 77
nuts. *see also* peanuts
    about, 8
    Arugula Almond Not-Pesto, 75
    Marjoram Walnut Not-Pesto, 74
    Mint Pistachio Not-Pesto, 77
    Nut Salsas and Sauces, 130–134, *131–133*

O
oils, about, 7, 11
onions and onion rings. *see also* scallions
    Cheesy Onion Bread Pudding, 17
    Gluten-Free Not-Rings, 89
    Onion Panade, *13,* 16
    Onion Ringings, about, 86
    Regular Onions with Hoisin and Shaoxing Wine, 85
    Yogurt Rings, 88

P
packaged foods, 35–61. *see also* enhanced dishes
    about, 36–38
    Cannellini Bean and Celery Salad with Anchovies, 51
    Can of Beans Cooked with Rice and Lots of Scallions and Cilantro, 52
    Chickpeas with Tomato, Rosemary, and Cream, 53
    eggs, about, 59
    The Garbonanza MUFU: Chickpea with Turmeric and Cilantro, 48, *49*
    Hackaroni and Cheese, 43–44
    Hamburg-A-Roni: Campfire Edition, 57–58, *58*
    instant soup, 39–40
    mash-up fry-ups (MUFUs), about, 45
    The Mitts-Full MUFU: Can of Corn *and* Can of Black Beans, 46
    Pasta with Sardines, 56
    popcorn, 38–39
    Red Bean MUFU: Smoky Style, 50
    Sardine and Anchovy S'cool, about, 54
    Spaghetti with Cream, Garlic, and Anchovies, 55
    Tortilla Española on Vacation, 60, *61*
    Vegetable Soup with Cauliflower, Apple, Peas, and Spices, *41,* 41–42
    White Bean MUFU: Tuscan Style, 47
Pancakes, Mushy Rice, 31, *32–33*
Parmesan, about, 11
parsley
    about, 7
    Broccoli with Parsley, Feta, and Black Pepper, pureed, 128
pasta
    Hackaroni and Cheese, 43–44
    Pasta with Sardines, 56
    Penne in Pink, 137
    Spaghetti with Cream, Garlic, and Anchovies, 55
peanuts
    Cilantro Peanut Not-Pesto, 76
    in Nut Salsas and Sauces, 130
    Swooshes with Peanuts and Ginger, 90

peas
    Mac and Peas (and bacon), 44
    Peas with Sage and Mint, or with Cumin and
        Coriander, pureed, 128
    Vegetable Soup with Cauliflower, Apple, Peas,
        and Spices, *41*, 41–42
popcorn, 38–39
Pork Etcetrazzini, Vindaloo-Style, 26–28. *see also*
    bacon, pork, and sausage
Potatoes, Baked, and Surrogate Fries, 103

R
Radishes, Roasted, with Chiles, Lime, and Fish
    Sauce, 94, 95
Ranch Dressing, 71
Really Boiled Vegetables, 23
Really Roasted Vegetables
    about, 18
    Roasted Vegetable Cornmeal Cakes, 19
    Roasted Vegetable Salad with Figgy Dressing,
        22
    Roasted Vegetable Salad with Ginger, Lime,
        and Sour Cream, 20, *21*
Really Well-Done Meats
    about, 24
    Cheesy Chicken Etcetrazzini, 26
    Herby Beef Etcetrazzini, 26
    Lamb Leg Etcetrazzini, 28
    Turkey Etcetrazzini and variations, 25–28, *27*
    Vindaloo-Style Pork Etcetrazzini, 26–28
Red Bean MUFU: Smoky Style, 50
Red-Faced Old Man, 154
Regular Onions with Hoisin and Shaoxing Wine,
    85
rice
    Can of Beans Cooked with Rice and Lots of
        Scallions and Cilantro, 52
    Coconut Rice Pudding with Ginger, 30
    Mushy Rice, 29
    Mushy Rice Pancakes, 31, *32–33*
Roasted Radishes with Chiles, Lime, and Fish Sauce,
    94, 95
Roasted Vegetable Cornmeal Cakes, 19
Roasted Vegetable Salad with Figgy Dressing, 22
Roasted Vegetable Salad with Ginger, Lime, and
    Sour Cream, 20, *21*

S
Sardine and Anchovy S'cool. *see also* seafood
    about, 54
    Pasta with Sardines, 56
    Spaghetti with Cream, Garlic, and Anchovies,
        55
sauces and dips, 125–149
    about, 126
    Anchovy Butter, 147
    Brown Butters, 143
    butter, about, 142
    Butter Pan Sauce, 144
    Caper-Lemon Butter, 148
    chermoula in Carrots Roasted in the
        Aftermath, *98*, 99
    Chile-Lime Butter, 149
    Citrus Butter, 149
    compound butters, about, 145
    cream, about, 136
    Creamy Cabbage with Caraway Seeds, Dill,
        and Hot Pepper, 138, *139*
    Creamy Sweet Peppers with Seeds Not Their
        Own, *140*, 141
    Dip of Fools, 142
    Ginger Butter, 148
    Golden Spiced Butter, 147
    Green Garlic Butter, 146
    Herb Butter, 146
    Milo's Bean Dip, 68, *69*
    Nut Salsas and Sauces, 130–134, *131–133*
    Penne in Pink, 137
    Scallion Dip, 102
    Smashed Beans, 129
    Vegetable Purees, 126–128, *127*
    Yogurt Sauces, 134, *135*
scallions
    Can of Beans Cooked with Rice and Lots of
        Scallions and Cilantro, 52
    Mess of Scallions, *100*, 101
    Scallion Dip, 102
seafood. *see also* anchovies
    Pasta with Sardines, 56
    Roasted Radishes with Chiles, Lime, and Fish
        Sauce, 94, 95
    Sardine and Anchovy S'cool, about,
        54

Unthick Clam Chowder: New England
    Version, Diner Version, 78–79
sesame seeds, about, 8
Skaket Beach Thins, 87
Smashed Beans, 129
soups
    instant, 39–40
    with Mushy Rice, 29
    with *Really* Boiled Vegetables, 23
    Unthick Clam Chowder: New England
        Version, Diner Version, 78–79
    Vegetable Soup with Cauliflower, Apple, Peas,
        and Spices, *41*, 41–42
Sour Old Man, 154
Spaghetti with Cream, Garlic, and Anchovies, 55
Spice-Encrusted BS Chicken Breast Roast, 116
spices, about, 8. *see also* herbs and spices
Sweet Old Man, 154

T

Tortilla Española on Vacation, 60, *61*
Turkey Etcetrazzini and variations, 25–28, *27*
turmeric
    about, 8–9
    BS Chicken Breast, Tangy and Turmerical, 115
    The Garbonanza MUFU: Chickpea with
        Turmeric and Cilantro, 48, *49*

U

Unthick Clam Chowder: New England Version,
    Diner Version, 78–79

V

vegetables, 81–103. *see also individual names of
    vegetables*
    about, 82
    Baked Potatoes and Surrogate Fries, 103
    Brocco Tacos, 83–84
    Carrots Roasted in the Aftermath, *98, 99*
    Celery Baked with Black Pepper, Bacon, and
        Cream, *92, 93*

Celery Swooshes with Peanuts and Ginger, 90
Glazed Carrot Phalanges (A.K.A. Baby
    Carrots), *96, 97*
Gluten-Free Not-Rings, 89
in Hackaroni and Cheese, 44
Mess of Scallions, *100*, 101
Mushrooms with Honey and Coriander, 91
Onion Ringings, about, 86
Really Boiled Vegetables, 23
Really Roasted Vegetables, 18
Regular Onions with Hoisin and Shaoxing
    Wine, 85
Roasted Radishes with Chiles, Lime, and Fish
    Sauce, 94, 95
Roasted Vegetable Cornmeal Cakes, 19
Roasted Vegetable Salad with Figgy Dressing,
    22
Roasted Vegetable Salad with Ginger, Lime,
    and Sour Cream, 20, *21*
Scallion Dip, 102
Skaket Beach Thins, 87
Vegetable Purees, 126–128, *127*
Vegetable Soup with Cauliflower, Apple, Peas,
    and Spices, Knorr version, *41*, 42
Vegetable Soup with Cauliflower, Apple, Peas,
    and Spices, scratch version, 42
Yogurt Rings, 88
Vindaloo-Style Pork Etcetrazzini, 26–28

W

Wesley Hackaroni and Cheese, 43–44
White Bean MUFU: Tuscan Style, 47
Winter Squash with Cardamom, pureed, 128
Wise Old Man, 155

Y

Yogurt Rings, 88
Yogurt Sauces, 134, *135*

HarperCollins books may be purchased for educational, business, or sales promotional use. For information, please email the Special Markets Department at SPsales@harpercollins.com.

FIRST EDITION

DESIGNED BY RENATA DE OLIVEIRA

Photographs by Liam Peternell

Illustrations by Liam Peternell, Milo Henderson, Hop Peternell, Kathleen Henderson, and Cal Peternell

Library of Congress Cataloging-in-Publication Data

Names: Peternell, Cal, author.
Title: Burnt toast and other disasters : a book of heroic hacks, fabulous
    fixes, and secret sauces / Cal Peternell.
Description: First edition. | New York : William Morrow, an imprint of
    HarperCollins Publishers, [2021] | Includes index. | Summary: "A gifty,
    funny, and practical guide to coming back from even the worst kitchen
    mistakes, making bad food good and making good food better, from the
    author of the *New York Times* bestselling and IACP Award–winning *Twelve
    Recipes*"— Provided by publisher.
Identifiers: LCCN 2021014651 | ISBN 9780062986740 | ISBN 9780062986757
    (ebook)
Subjects: LCSH: Cooking. | LCGFT: Cookbooks.
Classification: LCC TX714 .P46226 2021 | DDC 641.5—dc23
LC record available at https://lccn.loc.gov/2021014651

ISBN 978-0-06-298674-0

21 22 23 24 25   WOR   10 9 8 7 6 5 4 3 2 1